MOTHER TERESA

Inspirations From A Friend

HANNELORE ANGELA BENJAMIN

MOTHER TERESA - *Inspirations From A Friend.*

Front cover photo credit: © 1986 Túrelio (via Wikimedia-Commons), 1986

Hardcover edition published by BookBaby
7905 N Crescent Blvd, Pennsauken Township, NJ 08110

Book edited by McDonald P. Benjamin
Book designed by Alessandra Benjamin

ISBN 978-1-66789-024-1

ACKNOWLEDGEMENTS

This book is written in memory of the most extraordinary and inspiring missionary of all times: Mother Teresa, the motherly saint and humanitarian, who brought love, help and hope to the poor in the slums of Calcutta and to children all around the world.

This book is also dedicated to my late husband, Ambassador Dr. McDonald P. Benjamin, who devoted his life to eradicating hunger and poverty in the world's poorest countries, and who was my mentor and my best friend.

I am also deeply grateful to my children, McDonald and Sandra, for their love, patience and constant support. Both are the light of my life.

Finally, my debt of gratitude goes to Pegi Deitz Shae, distinguished publicist and writer, for her help, patience and professional advice. Without her, I might never have completed this manuscript.

Hannelore Angela Benjamin

Alexandria, Virginia, February 2020

CONTENTS

INTRODUCTION

*"The destitute, the hungry, sick and poor have the right
to die with dignity."*

Mother Teresa

I am Hannelore Angela Benjamin, born in Germany and married to
the late Ambassador Dr. McDonald Phillip Benjamin. I have two
wonderful children, McDonald Jr. and Sandra. They are true friends to
me and they provided patient and continuous support as I wrote about
Mother Teresa.

I had the privilege of meeting Mother Teresa on three occasions,
and we talked for many hours with no cameras and no people to
disturb us. Our conversations were not just lively banter but rather
heart-to-heart conversations. My heart still stirs when I think back
to our meetings, to her stories about her life, and to her dreams. The
following pages cannot fully convey all that we discussed. However,
I have tried to share as many facets as possible, and to go beyond
another biography of Mother Teresa by expressing how she felt and
thought, in particular when she was away from Calcutta. Hopefully I
can convey some of the light, humor and warmth of her personality,

as well as her complete dedication to her divinely inspired mission. Mother Teresa had an incredible determination and a strong will. She felt she was a soul with a mission. Her deep devotion to God and to Jesus and her belief in Mary, the Mother of Jesus, helped her achieve her goal in life, namely to become a missionary dedicated completely to helping the poor, the hungry and the sick in the slums of Calcutta, India.[1]

I remember her hands holding mine; they were thin and gnarled, yet very soft and strong. It was incredible to think that those same hands had picked up unwanted babies and desperately sick people in the slums to carry them lovingly to her Missionaries of Charity in Calcutta, so as to offer some of the most vulnerable people on earth medical help, food, shelter, dignity and love. I can still see her face filled with deep wrinkles before me. Each line told the story of her life, her hard work and suffering, her constant travels, and her compassion for those living in abject poverty and abandonment. And yet I never heard her complain, for her devotion to Jesus guided all that she did and helped her to overcome the countless challenges that she faced. I remember her telling me how she did not always sense His presence at her side, but that she had complete faith that He was guiding all her work, and that she always looked to see Him in the people she served.

In the following chapters I will try to tell the story about the real Mother Teresa, the Mother Teresa whose eyes brimmed with sincerity, intelligence and a little mischief when she told me about her path in life, and the Mother Teresa who touched my hand with the compassion of a true friend when she felt my sadness.

---

1. The city of Calcutta in the Indian state of Bengal was renamed Kolkata in 2001, however as Mother Teresa is widely known in English as Mother Teresa of Calcutta, I have continued to use the earlier name for the city here.

It is Mother Teresa who inspired me to write this book, and in particular to share with you three key messages that she shared with me, imbued as they are with her love, faith and compassion. Her moving words remain an inspiration to me in so many ways. When I told her I wanted to write about her, I remember the twinkle in her eyes as she said: "But I want to have the first copy!"

When Mother Teresa told me her story, she admitted that at first her path was not easy, but that God gave her the strength to keep advancing in her mission. And so it has been, in its own way, with this book too. While I have written some fiction stories in the past, especially for children, this is the first time I am writing a non-fiction book, and in this case with all the aches and pains of my old age. I give thanks to God for His support, without which I would not have been able to complete this book for you.

It is my hope that, drawing on my personal conversations with Mother Teresa, this book will be very different from the many biographies that chronicle Mother Teresa's life, by bringing out aspects of her character that others may not have highlighted, sources of inspiration in the saints that went before her, friendships that she treasured, and messages that she left for me. Our lives became linked through our friendship, and in sharing this book with you I have tried to be true to that friendship. If I have unwittingly made some mistakes in the process, I ask for your kind forgiveness.

Hannelore Angela Benjamin

MOTHER TERESA'S PRAYER

"People are often unreasonable, illogical and self-centered.

Forgive them anyway.

If you are kind, people may accuse you of selfish ulterior motives.

Be kind anyway.

If you are successful, you will win some unfaithful friends and

some genuine enemies.

Succeed anyway.

If you are honest and sincere, people may deceive you.

Be honest and sincere anyway.

What you spend years creating, others could destroy overnight.

Create anyway.

If you find serenity and happiness, some may be jealous.

Be happy anyway.

The good you do today will often be forgotten.

Do good anyway.

Give the best you have, and it will never be enough.

Give your best anyway.

In the final analysis, it is between you and God.

It was never between you and them anyway."

Mother Teresa

CHAPTER I

MOTHER TERESA AND I MEET FOR THE FIRST TIME

"Pray to Mary the Mother of Jesus whenever you are in need. She will be there to help."

Mother Teresa

TRAVELLING FROM LONDON TO ROME

One sunny day back in 1980, I flew from London's Heathrow airport to Rome's Fiumicino airport. When I boarded the plane, I did not realize that that day would be a special day, indeed a blessed day for me. I am still filled with gratitude to God for what happened that day.

I entered the plane and went to my seat, which was an aisle seat in the first row of Economy, right behind First Class. There was no one seated in the middle seat. I stood up when a small, distinguished person, dressed in a sari, came down the aisle and the flight attendant guided her to the window seat in my row. It could not be! It was… Mother Teresa! And there was no one else seated between her and me! I could not believe the privilege that I was being given. There I was, sitting next to Mother Teresa in person! ME! It was an opportunity not too many people would ever experience.

Before long we were engaged in the most interesting conversation, the kind of conversation that two strangers seldom have. Luckily, during the entire flight we were never disturbed by other passengers, and thanks to this precious one-on-one time for the full flight of almost three hours, I got to know Mother Teresa in the most incredible way.

How can I describe it? Well, in talking with and listening to her, I understood that Mother Teresa was filled with the wisdom of the humble and with the quiet, relentless determination of a person on a mission since her youth, inspired as she was by her deep devotion and love for Jesus and for Mother Mary. She had the most wonderful dry sense of humor and displayed an incredible inner strength and charisma.

By nature, we were both reserved people, and yet we felt very comfortable with each other, so we talked comfortably with each other about our lives. I can still hear Mother Teresa asking me:

"Angela, what are you doing with your life?"

"Mother Teresa," I answered. "I am the President of the United Nations Women's Guild (UNWG) in Rome. Our Guild is devoted to helping the neediest children around the world. Through donations, bazaars and various other events, we are able to raise funds to help needy children in Asia and the Near East, Africa, and Latin America and the Caribbean."

"How do you help them?" She asked. I gave her several examples of the work we did through the UNWG.

"In Bangladesh, we helped eight blind boys to be operated for cataracts. After the surgeries, all eight boys could, for the very first time, see their parents, their siblings, the nature that surrounded them, and the sun, moon and stars! In Brazil, we sent artificial skin for indigenous children who had fallen into a fire pit. With the artificial skin their faces were restored to a certain extent. In the case of the Sahel zone in Africa, we sent two Braille machines for blind people, so that teenagers could learn how to use them and be able to make a living. We also helped to train blind people to make handicrafts for a living. In Nepal, we supported the construction of a well to make water more easily available for people from five villages, so that they would no longer have to walk for hours to get water. We did the same in Bhutan and in other countries. In India, poor mothers received stoves so that they would be able not only to cook meals for their families but also to sell food on the streets. They also received sewing machines to sew clothes that they could sell. The list of ideas for projects that we receive and review at the Board of the United Nations Women's Guild (UNWG) is endless and it never gets shorter!"

As we both laughed, Mother Teresa said: "I know what you mean with the endless list, but it is good to see that you do so much to help the poor." I could see that she was truly touched as she listened to me, because in a deeply personal way she knew and felt the pain of the needy, and she knew the joy they felt in being supported with love.

I told Mother Teresa how my support for needy children had begun a long time ago: "In 1964, when I was living in Panama, some friends from the diplomatic corps and I decided to help the nuns at a convent in Panama City. Every day, about thirty children who lived in the city's slums would come to the convent to hear the word of God. We used these meetings to teach them how to sew nightshirts and decorate them with simple embroidery. They also learnt to wash their hands before eating and to keep themselves clean. We volunteers would also accompany the nuns to the poorest sections of Panama City to give babies Vitamin A supplements on their tongues, weigh and clean the babies, and to give the toddlers little handmade toys. It was very inspiring for us to be able to help them."

Listening to my stories, Mother Teresa's eyes started to shine, as if they were filled with tears that she did not shed. She did not want the tears to come. She began to tell me about her life. She shared how she felt when she left her family and friends, and she talked about her homesickness. Mother Teresa reminisced about her long journey from Skopje in Macedonia to Paris, France, and then on to the Loreto Abbey and Mother House in Rathfarnham, Dublin, Ireland, whence she left for Calcutta by boat. She also told me about her life in Calcutta and how the work expanded to other parts of India and beyond. I also spoke to her about my life, first in Germany, then in the United States and in Rome, Italy. The sharing of our personal stories began when I said to her:

"Mother Teresa, in my youth I was a real tomboy; no water was too deep for me to swim in and no tree too high for me to climb! Although I belonged to the St. Michael's Church Choir and I loved to sing, I also loved downhill skiing and playing tennis. I also played the harmonica, which I'm sure got on a lot of people's nerves!"

Mother Teresa laughed softly and replied: "Angela, you know, when I was very young, I was a tomboy too! My brother could have told quite some stories about me!"

"Not you, Mother Teresa?!" I exclaimed.

"Yes, me!" she replied, and continued chuckling. "I too loved to sing and to play the mandolin. On Sundays, my mother would take us to our village church for Mass. Actually, even now I sometimes sing to myself."

"Please tell me, Mother Teresa, how did you become such a devoted missionary? What brought you to this path?"

She looked out the window for a short while, as if she had entered a world of her own for a moment where no one could follow her, before she turned back towards me and told me the most wonderful story of her life.

"When I was a young girl, a Jesuit priest in our community, Father Jambrekovic, told me stories about India. He told me about the destitute, the lepers and those who did not know about the word of God. I kept thinking about his stories, and told my mother everything he had said. I told her that when I grew up I wanted to go to India and help the poor and destitute and homeless. I told her I wanted to become a missionary. My mother was a very holy person and always tried to help our neighbors, so I think she understood me. I remember she stroked my hair and said: 'We will see'.

"Later I spoke about it with Father Jambrekovic. He was a little hesitant when he heard what I intended to do, but he listened to me with patience. He would often sit with me and explain to me that it would be hard to become a missionary in India."

Mother Teresa took a deep breath and then continued.

"Angela, it was not easy to take the decision to leave my family and friends to go to India. We were a very happy family and a very united family, so it was a big sacrifice to leave them. Also, I did not speak any English – only Serbo-Croat and Albanian – so how was I going to communicate? I asked myself this many times, and in fact I had many questions with no answers. But my mind was made up. Every day I asked God for help.

"Then the day came when my mother, my sister Aga and I, left our home and we went from Skopje to Belgrade and then on to Zagreb. There I had to say good-bye to my mother and my sister. It was very hard, because I did not know if we would ever see each other again. In Zagreb, I was glad to meet up with Betike Kanje, who travelled onwards with me. She is a very dear person. She too wanted to become a missionary and we became good friends and traveled together by train through Austria and onto Paris."

Mother Teresa paused quietly for a moment, as if lost in her memories. Then when she turned to me again, I told her that I had also been to Belgrade, Zagreb and Slovenia and to other parts of the former Yugoslavia.

"Tell me about it, Angela, tell me!"

And so I told her about the lovely cathedrals, churches and a museum that I had visited, and about the nice people I had met. Mother Teresa was touched and her eyes looked moist. I patted her hand to comfort her. She smiled at me, and for a moment we remained silent. There were no words spoken. We just looked at each other and understood each other. Then she shook her head briefly and continued her story:

"Angela, when we arrived in Paris, we were met by two Sisters from the House of Loreto, who took us to the Loreto Abbey. The Mother Superior welcomed us and interviewed us to make certain that we really wanted to become missionaries and that we were really ready to devote our life to God. After a couple of days in Paris, we traveled on to the Mother House in Rathfarnham, which is in Dublin, Ireland. We were excited about going to the Mother House. That is where we began to learn English and to learn more about serving as missionaries."

I reflected on what she said. It brought back memories of my own, and so I said to her: "Do you know, Mother Teresa, that in 1961 I too left my home town in Germany and all my family and friends? I went to America, where a friend of mine lived. I was scared when I saw all those tall skyscrapers in New York, and I was overwhelmed by the massive crowds of people and by so many big cars in the streets, all the traffic and all those bright lights. I too spoke very little English at the time."

Mother Teresa nodded her head. She understood me.

"Mother Teresa," I said. "Can you please tell me about your time in Rathfarnham, and about your life in Calcutta? Please forgive me if I am asking too many questions!"

"Don't worry, Angela. In fact, I enjoy speaking about the Mother House in Rathfarnham! I was happy there. In fact I went back to visit them a few years ago, you know? And Calcutta…" Mother Teresa paused in contemplation for a moment. "There is so much to say about Calcutta!" She then took my hand and patted it briefly and said: "But first let us pray."

Mother Teresa held her Rosary in her hands, closed her eyes and began to pray to Mary, the Mother of Jesus. When I saw her praying the Rosary, I also reached into my handbag and drew out the Rosary that I always carry with me and I joined her in prayer. In fact, I must confess that I peeked to see which Rosary bead she was on so that I could move my hands quickly to the same bead on my Rosary! After she finished her prayers, she looked at me and saw that I was holding a Rosary in my hands. She then asked me about my religion, and I explained to her that I had been raised as a Roman Catholic and that my family was strictly Catholic. Mother Teresa nodded her head and said:

"I am happy to hear that."

Then she looked at me quietly and smiled…It was in that special moment that I knew that we were two people who truly appreciated and respected each other and that we were beginning to form a friendship that could last for a lifetime.

Then Mother Teresa told me her stories about her trip first to Rathfarnham and then on to India, and about her life and work in India and beyond (shared in the chapters below), and I was enthralled as I listened to her. There was so much love in her stories, and alas, so much anguish. My heart went out to all the suffering people whom she had met and helped in Calcutta. I felt like I was walking with her along those narrow streets, meeting the sick and the vulnerable, by day or by night, in the poorest parts of Calcutta. She spoke so simply and yet so vividly. As she talked, I felt the joys and the fears of accompanying her to serve the poorest of the poor.

All that time, while I delighted in this private conversation with Mother Teresa and in the stories she told me, most other people in the aircraft did not even realize that she was on the plane! The flight attendants left us alone most of the time. When they served us our lunch, we prayed and thanked God for the food. As the flight attendant withdrew our trays, Mother Teresa softly asked her if she could have the orange juices of the passengers who did not want theirs, if the juices were still sealed. Mother Teresa told the flight attendant that she wanted to take them to her Missionaries of Charity to give them to the poor. I was struck by how at every moment, even on a flight from London to Rome, Mother Teresa was thinking about the poor and how she could help them! I quickly gave her my orange juice too!! Later, after arriving at Fiumicino airport in Rome, the flight attendant brought a large bag of orange juices down the steps onto the tarmac and gave it to an official from the Vatican who was waiting for Mother Teresa, so that she could take the orange juices with her.

As I look back on those precious moments on the flight with Mother Teresa, I wonder whether I can ever describe the wonderful feelings that went through me, the deep sense of peace, or the humbling experience of being in her company, praying the Rosary with her, and seeing how completely she was dedicated to her mission and how all-embracing her love was. I don't believe I truly can do justice to those sentiments in these pages, but these feelings are embedded in my heart and mind forever.

Before we landed, Mother Teresa wrote down her address for me so that we could remain in contact by mail. As I look back now, it is hard to believe how much harder it was back then to remain in contact: we had no email, no internet or Wi-Fi or social media, and international telephone calls were extremely expensive. But that also allows me to look back instead, even today, on the handwritten note that Mother Teresa gave me (see the photograph below), in ways that bring back many more memories.

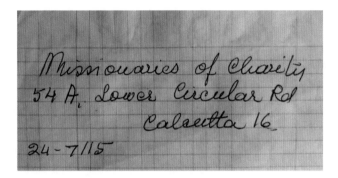

ON THE TARMAC IN ROME

The plane had circled over Rome a few times before descending. After landing, it rolled slowly over the tarmac and taxied to a stop near the main terminal building. We had arrived at Fiumicino airport. I walked down the stairs of the airplane behind Mother Teresa and onto the tarmac, holding her bag for her. A car from the Vatican was waiting for her on the tarmac.

She turned around to me to say farewell. Her last words to me before she left me that day were: "Angela, friends do not need to meet all the time. It is comforting to know that they are there in times of need. Please tell everyone you know to hold the poor close to their hearts. That is the wish of our beloved Jesus."

Then Mother Teresa reached up and made the sign of the cross on my forehead.

I nodded to her, and whispered a quiet thank you. I was too overcome with emotions to be able to speak.

Standing there on the tarmac, I waved farewell to Mother Teresa and the emissary from the Vatican. Slowly the car drove away, yet I kept on waving. That day I did not know if we would ever meet again.

Suddenly it all seemed so unreal. I could not believe that I, of all people, had had the privilege of meeting one of the most loving and humanitarian people of all times. I had met 'the' Mother Teresa, who devoted herself to helping the destitute and sick in Calcutta. The Mother Teresa of the Slums. I had been able to talk and pray with her for around three hours on the plane with nobody to disturb us, even though the plane was filled with passengers.

Was it really only moments ago that I had said good-bye to her? I could still feel her hand holding mine: small, strong and gnarled, although it felt soft when she said good-bye to me and made the sign of the cross on my forehead. I felt humbled, and blessed and inspired with a renewed energy to help the poor, especially through my work at the United Nations Women's Guild. Looking up at the sky, all I could say was: "Thank you, God."

CHAPTER II

MOTHER TERESA AND I MEET FOR THE SECOND TIME

"Believe in God and trust in Him, for He is
at your side all the time."

Mother Teresa

AT THE MISSIONARIES OF CHARITY IN ROME

We did meet a second time! It was in the spring of 1981, the sun was out and the air was crisp that day, filled with the fragrance of flowers and the chirping of birds.

Mother Teresa had flown into Rome to meet with Pope John Paul II. He had sent her an airplane ticket to visit him in Rome, as he wanted to talk with her about an important matter. Mother Teresa also had to attend various other important meetings. As always, she was staying at her Missionaries of Charity in Piazza San Gregorio on the Palatine Hill, overlooking the famous Ancient Roman chariot-racing stadium, the *Circus Maximus*.

Knowing that Mother Teresa was in Rome, I had called her and she had suggested that we get together at her Missionaries of Charity in Rome, and had proposed the day and time.

Two members of the Board of Directors of the United Nations Women's Guild accompanied me to the Missionaries of Charity. One of Mother Teresa's missionaries opened the door and led us to their simple meeting room. After a while, Mother Teresa joined us and the four of us had a nice conversation. I had brought a check with a donation from the UNWG for Mother Teresa to help the children in Calcutta through her Missionaries of Charity. Together with my Board members, I gave her the check and told her that our organization wanted to support the work of the Missionaries of Charity more. Mother Teresa was very grateful to us for the donation, assuring us that it would go to support the poorest of the poor.

After we all spoke together for a few more moments, to my surprise, Mother Teresa took me by the hand and led me out into the garden. I cannot describe how humbled I was, and at the same time how very special I felt. My heart filled with excitement and gratitude! I still remember the strength and warmth that she exuded as her small, gnarled, gentle and yet strong fingers curled around mine. I kept thinking to myself: 'How can such small hands lift up the people in the slums of Calcutta?' I was amazed.

I cannot remember whether the garden was big or small; I only saw Mother Teresa, and a little chirping sparrow! It flew from tree to tree, following us. We both laughed and joked that: "It is curious and wants to listen to us!"

My heart was pounding with joy as we talked about her Missionaries, her friendship with Pope John Paul II, what had inspired her to do the work that she did, and about her devotion to Jesus and to Mary, the Mother of Jesus.

Her eyes brimmed with sincerity, alternating between a humorous twinkle and an occasional wistful pensiveness, especially when she reflected compassionately on the people she had devoted her life to serving. I felt privileged by the sincere friendship and the trust she placed in me as she talked about the sources of inspiration that had led her to the point we were that day, and in turn I shared, with an open and grateful heart, the stories that had shaped my life. We never realized that time was flying by – we were in our own moment in time, as we walked back and forth in the garden, much of the time holding hands, and talked and talked and talked.

As we talked about our backgrounds, Mother Teresa took my hand and chuckled, saying: "You know, by blood I am Albanian, by birth I am a Macedonian, by faith I am a Catholic, and by citizenship I am Indian! And you?"

"Mother Teresa, by birth I am German, I live here in Rome and I am a devoted Roman Catholic. I am married to a Dominican, and I have two wonderful children; one is German and the other is American!"

We both chuckled.

"Are you happy to be here in Rome?" I asked.

"Yes. As you know, I have come to see His Holiness the Pope," she said, and then added: "Rome is a beautiful city." We talked about the catacombs where the early Christians buried their dead underground and found they could also worship freely without fear of persecution. Nowadays, tourists still stream to the Catacombs of St. Callixtus located on the Appian Way, which today still has segments of the old Roman road with large cobblestones laid two millennia ago.

We talked about the Archbasilica of St. John of Lateran, the oldest public church in Rome and the seat of the Pope as Bishop of

Rome. We talked about the Vatican and the Swiss Guards who guard it. They are a highly dedicated elite force but are best known for their Renaissance-era uniforms in the red, yellow and blue colors of the Medici family.[2] And Mother Teresa and I talked about Michelangelo's famous marble sculpture, "*La Pietá*", in the Vatican, in which Mary looks down in mourning on Jesus as she cradles his body in her arms just after he has been lowered down from the cross. Mother Teresa and I shared how we were both moved by the beauty of this statue, and by the love of Mary and the sacrifice of Jesus that it displays.

Michelangelo's "*La Pietá*"[3]

---

2 Image by Daniela Mackova from Pixabay, accessed on 7th November, 2019, available at: https://pixabay.com/photos/swiss-guards-basilica-soldier-rome-1341299/.

3 Photo credit: Tim Stringer, available on Pixabay, accessed on 29th October, 2019 at: https://pixabay.com/photos/la-pieta-rome-st-peter-s-vatican-2245826/.

"Mother Teresa," I asked at one point. "Please forgive me for asking you, but can you please tell me again what really inspired you to become a missionary?"

"Of course," she said. She thought for a moment, and then continued: "Ever since I was a young child and could read, I read about St. Francis and his life, about how he helped poor and hungry people. It was he in particular, as well as St. Thérèse of Lisieux and St. Joan of Arc who inspired me. They were devoted to God. Only St. Thérèse was not allowed to go out and help the poor as she had hoped she would be able to. She did not have the freedom to do so. It was a different time. And Joan of Arc heard the word of God and had the faith and the courage to follow His word as a young woman at a very difficult time."

I listened to her speaking about her sources of inspiration and pondered about how they had influenced her life. I then asked her: "You have established many Missionaries of Charity around the world. How did you manage to do that?"

"It was not easy," she replied. "I have to travel constantly to find funds, to build the Missions and to take care of all the devoted Sisters who are doing such blessed work. Visiting other countries is also nice, since I can talk to people about God's love for them, and tell those who do not know about Him about the life and love of Jesus. The work we do is a means to put our love for Jesus into action."

"Mother Teresa, I find it so beautiful and so moving that you have been able to help so many poor, sick and hungry people."

"God has been with me at every step," she replied. "His Grace has helped me to bring His love to many people. You know, Angela, there is no greater poverty than feeling unwanted. Many of the people whom our Missionaries care for felt unwanted and forgotten by their families and society. Every one wants and deserves to feel loved, and that love should begin in their homes, but it is not always that way.

"Unfortunately, often we reach people when they are already very ill and all we can do is hold their hands and pray for them, but even that can be important for someone, because everyone has a right to die with dignity."

"There are so many needy people in so many countries. How have you been able to find funds to help so many people?" I asked.

With a twinkle in her eyes she told me: "When I travel, I never stop asking for funds and I never feel too proud to do so. Yet, Angela, when I walk in the neighborhoods where the poorest of the poor live, I never think about whether I can help one or two or three people. For me it is important just to be able to help the person in front of me. I can only help one person at a time. We must not try to do big or extraordinary things. We must simply help those who are close to us and put extraordinary love into the little things that we can do for them. Sometimes all that we can do is to hold their hands, dry their tears, smile and comfort them, and pray for them in their last hour of life."

As I looked back later on our conversation, I sensed that she felt truly comfortable sharing her thoughts openly with me. I was not interviewing her and there were no cameras flashing. There were just two people with a love of Jesus and a wish to serve, who were sharing their thoughts. I would read in the media later that Mother Teresa was very shy, but the Mother Teresa I got to know was not shy. No, in her vocation to serve God and help the needy, she simply did not want the public spotlight to be on her, but rather on the unfulfilled and so often ignored needs of the poorest of the poor.

I said to Mother Teresa: "You know, our organization would like to give more to support your work, but there are financial restrictions here in Italy that make it difficult to send money abroad."

"Angela, that is not a problem. Our Missionaries of Charity are a Pontifical congregation and we have accounts at the Vatican Bank. I will introduce you to Archbishop Marcinkus. He is the President of the Vatican Bank. Before you leave I will give you his direct telephone number. Please go and see him."

"Thank you, Mother Teresa, I will call Monsignor Marcinkus in the next few days to see if I can meet with him."

Whenever Mother Teresa spoke about God or her special friends, there was a special luminosity in her eyes. They would fill with a warm glow, a smile would form on her lips and her voice would resonate softly.

That afternoon, Mother Teresa shared many more words with me that will always remain dear to me. Many of the words of wisdom that she shared that afternoon, as well as on our flight from London to Rome, will appear in the following chapters of this simple book. A few words will remain just for our selves.

At the end of our conversation, we said a small prayer together and then went to join the two Board members from the UNWG who had been waiting inside for us.

Saying good-bye to Mother Teresa, I felt sad to leave, and yet I felt blessed at the same time, for our friendship had deepened and I knew we shared a uniquely special bond of friendship. Mother Teresa and I had become truly trusting friends, with a bond of friendship built on mutual respect, trust, understanding and appreciation, and on our shared devotion to God.

Mother Teresa in Rome at the Missionaries of Charity[4]

---

4 This wonderful picture of Mother Teresa laughing, just as we had laughed together, was taken during another visit by her to her Missionaries of Charity in Rome, just four years after we had met there. Photo credit: Manfredo Ferrari [CC BY-SA 4.0 (https://creativecommons.org/licenses/by-sa/4.0)], available at: https://commons.wikimedia.org/wiki/File:Mutter Teresa von Kalkutta.jpg, accessed on 1st June, 2019. There are many publications with beautiful illustrations and photographs of the life of Mother Teresa. As an example, see the photographic record compiled by Michael Collopy, entitled: "Works of Love are Works of Peace: Mother Teresa and the Missionaries of Charity", published by Ignatius Press, San Francisco, 1996. Also see the Time Magazine Special Edition by David Biema entitled: "Mother Teresa: The Life and Works of a Modern Saint", published by Time Inc. Books, New York, 2016.

CHAPTER III

EARLY SOURCES OF INSPIRATION FOR MOTHER TERESA

*"I beseech thee, O Lord, that the fiery and
sweet strength of Thy love may absorb my soul
from all things that are under heaven"*

Saint Francis of Assisi

*"The good God does not need years to accomplish His
work of love in a soul; One ray from His Heart can, in an
instant, make His flower bloom for eternity."*

Saint Thérèse of Lisieux

*I place trust in God, my creator, in all things; I love Him
with all my heart."*

Saint Joan of Arc

SAINT FRANCIS OF ASSISI

During our walk in the gardens of the Missionaries of Charity in Rome, Mother Teresa and I shared many stories about our lives. In the course of our conversation, I asked Mother Teresa:

"Mother Teresa, who inspired you when you were young?"

"Saint Francis inspired me deeply, Angela. I read about his devotion to God, and how fervently he loved Him. He lived the most humble life because he served the poor, and in fact rich people, including his father, looked down upon him, for Saint Francis had a heart for the poor and used all his money to help them. His life touched me, and even today he continues to inspire many people."[5]

As many readers may know, Saint Francis was born in Assisi, Italy in 1181.[6] His mother wanted to name him Giovanni, after Saint John the Baptist, however his father, Pietro Bernardone, who was a well-to-do merchant, did not want his son to be named after Saint John, and named him Francesco (Francis) instead. Pietro not only refused that his son be named after an apostle of Jesus, but also refused his son's wish to become a minister of God.

5 The picture of Saint Francis reproduced here is a famous painting by the 13th century Italian artist Cimabue that can be seen in the lower church of the Basilica of St. Francis in Assisi. Photo credit: https://search. creativecommons.org/photos/de64ef7b-7c68-420d-9cf1-b89f6fb114bb

6 There are many rich biographies of Saint Francis of Assisi. One of the earliest was written by Saint Bonaventure, a Franciscan theologian who was seven years old when Saint Francis of Assisi died. He wrote: *Legenda Sancti Franciscii*, or "The life of St. Francis of Assisi", which has been republished in 2010 by Tan Books, Charlotte, NC. A range of biographies of St. Francis are also available, including a succinct version

Once, when Francis was praying at the Church of San Damiano, he heard Jesus speaking to him, saying: "Francis, go and repair my church." Francis went to a small church that had been destroyed during the war between Assisi and Perugia and started to rebuild the church with his own hands. When Francis obeyed Jesus's wish, his friends, who shared his devotion, helped him, and when he had no money left, he used his father's money. Pietro became furious with his son and soon disinherited him.

After working on building his chapel for some time, Francis came to understand that he had misunderstood Jesus' words, and that what Jesus really wanted was for him to build a universal church, in the hearts of the people. Once he understood Jesus' message, Francis felt he was on a mission and started preaching the word of God to all who would listen to him. In 1210, he went to Rome to plead with Pope Innocent III to grant him permission to establish a new order, called the Brotherhood of Poverty. With the Pope's blessing, Francis established the Franciscan Order.

In all the pictures of Saint Francis, one sees him dressed in the simple brown habit of the Franciscan Order, holding a bird and flowers. He loved birds and was always surrounded by them, for they were never afraid of him, which attests to his goodness. Indeed Saint Francis came to be seen as the patron saint for animals and the environment. However, his primary mission, and the primary mission of his Order, was to attend to the poor and to minister to the faithful and bring them closer to God.

Saint Francis had a gift with words, and wherever he went, people came to listen to him preach. One young, well-respected

---

entitled "St. Francis of Assisi" by Catholic Online, available at: https://www.catholic.org/saints/saint. php?saint_id=50, accessed on 31st May, 2019.

woman named Claire heard him preach and wanted to follow him. One night, she and her sister Agnes left their parents' home and joined Saint Francis with two other friends. Saint Francis cut their hair and gave them Minorite habits with which they were to dress themselves. Francis then took them to the church of San Damian for shelter. San Damian had been given to him by the Benedictines and became the first monastery of the Franciscan Order.

Several legends arose around Saint Francis. In 1213, he traveled with his Franciscan Brothers to Bethlehem, because he wanted to see where Jesus was born. That visit inspired him to recreate the scene of the Nativity, and even today churches around the world follow his example by setting up Nativity scenes, with the one at the Cathedral in Assisi being one of the most beautiful ones. Legend has it that, on that visit to Bethlehem, Saint Francis also wanted to convert Muslims to Catholicism, and crossed enemy lines to meet with the Sultan of Egypt, who was so charmed by Saint Francis over several days of conversation that he wished to convert, but his position would not allow him to do so. Later, only Franciscans were allowed to be the custodians of Christian holy sites in Jerusalem.

In another legend, closer to home, there was a wolf that was terrorizing the people of the town of Gubbio. They called Saint Francis for help, and he went to Gubbio and confronted the wolf with just the gospel in his hand. According to the legend, Saint Francis told the wolf that it was not right to behave badly and scare the people, and asked him to repent, and the wolf listened to Saint Francis and never harmed the people again. Peace was restored in Gubbio, and in gratitude to Saint Francis, they placed a fresco over the altar of their main church showing Saint Francis and the wolf.

Toward the end of his life, as he became more and more ill, Francis prayed constantly to Jesus. Legend has it that, because he prayed so much to Jesus, in the end Saint Francis' hands were marked by the same wounds as Jesus had on the cross. Even when Saint Francis turned blind, he continued to preach the word of God. In 1228, two years after Saint Francis' death, Pope Gregory IX canonized him.

I could understand why Saint Francis was such a source of inspiration to Mother Teresa. I wish I could have told her that, many years later in 2011, my family and I visited the hilltop town of Assisi and attended Mass at the *Basilica Superiore di San Francesco d'Assisi*, which is the mother church of the Franciscan Order, where St. Francis was buried. Mother Teresa would have laughed if I had been able to tell her that my daughter Sandra had brought along a large bag to the Mass, filled with Italian coins, and that when a priest passed among the churchgoers during Mass to collect donations for the Church, Sandra tipped the entire bag of coins into the priest's collection basket! The priest looked at us in surprise and the basket became so heavy that the poor priest ended up dropping several of the coins on the floor of the church! We could not help smiling as he turned to walk away with the collection basket.

Then, little children sitting in the row in front of us quickly bent down to gather the coins for themselves, but were startled when one of the Franciscan nuns sitting in the row behind us lifted her forefinger and said to the children: "No, my little ones. Those coins belong to the church!" The little children turned red with shame, looked up at their parents, and then ran after the priest with the collection basket to give the coins to him. When the children returned, the nuns behind us smiled warmly at the children. Again, we too could not help smiling at the turn of events...

After the Mass ended, we lit several candles for the loved ones we had lost. One person I thought of as I lit the candles was Mother Teresa, for by the time my family and I visited St. Francis' Basilica in Assisi, the world had also lost Mother Teresa. She had been called back to God, just as in the final words of the famous prayer that Saint Francis left for us:

LORD,
make me an instrument of Your peace.
Where there is hatred, let me sow love;
Where there is injury, pardon;
Where there is doubt, faith;
Where there is despair, hope;
Where there is darkness, light,
And where there is sadness, joy.

DIVINE MASTER,
grant that I may not seek so much
To be consoled as to console;
To be understood as to understand;
To be loved as to love.
For it is in giving that we receive;
It is in pardoning that we ourselves are pardoned;
And it is in dying that we are born to eternal life.

Saint Francis of Assisi

SAINT THÉRÈSE OF LISIEUX

"You know, Angela," Mother Teresa said to me, as we walked through the gardens of the Missionaries of Charity in Rome. "When I chose my name Teresa, it was not because of St. Teresa of Avila, whom you know about, but of St. Thérèse of Lisieux, the little flower. She wanted to go out and help the poor but was not allowed to. I have been fortunate that God has given me that opportunity."

"So little Thérèse was a big inspiration?!" I asked, and we laughed.

Mother Teresa then replied: "St. Thérèse used to say that nothing is small in the eyes of God and that we should do everything that we do with love."

"That is so true," I replied, and we walked together quietly for a moment in thought.

Thérèse was born on January 2, 1873, at Alençon in Normandy, France, beforemoving with her family to Lisieux (also in Normandy) at the age of four. She was the ninth and the youngest child of Louis and Zélie Martin, who were devout Catholics. Unfortunately Thérèse's two brothers and two of her sisters died at a very young age, and indeed Thérèse's mother also died when Thérèse was only four years old. Thérèse's older sisters entered a Carmelite convent at a relatively early age, and Thérèse too devoted herself to God from a very young age, after she experienced a mystical visit by the infant Jesus on Christmas Eve in 1886.

At the age of fifteen, Thérèse asked for permission to enter the Carmelite

Convent too, but the Mother Superior argued that she was still too young to take the decision to devote her life to God.[7] In order to help Thérèse, her father, Louis, who nicknamed Thérèse "My Little Flower," went with her to Rome to ask permission directly of Pope Leo XIII. In her brief audience before the Pope, the Pope said she would do so if it were God's wish. Shortly thereafter, Bishop Hugonin, who was impressed by Thérèse's devotion to God, her courage and her desire to help the needy, gave his permission. He wrote to the Mother Superior on Thérèse's behalf and she finally consented to his request. Thérèse joined her elder sisters at the Carmelite convent on April 9, 1888.[8]

The convent turned out to be very different from what Thérèse had expected. She had wanted to go out and help the poor, but was forbidden to do so. Indeed, she had to adjust to the strict life of the convent and she became a cloistered nun. Years later she was placed in charge of all novices at the Convent.

When Thérèse became very ill at a fairly young age, her eldest sister, Mother Agnes, who was the Prioress at Thérèse's Carmelite convent, invited Thérèse to write a journal about her life, her love of and devotion to God, and her dreams to help the needy. Thérèse listened to her sister and, even in debilitatingly poor health, wrote three manuscripts about her feelings, hopes and wishes, before she died on September 30, 1897

---

7 The picture of Thérèse on the previous page shows her at the age of 15, just before she entered the Carmelite convent. It is available at: https://commons.wikimedia.org/wiki/File:Therese.jpg#filehistory, accessed on 1st June, 2019.

8 While there are several biographies about St. Thérèse of Lisieux, the best place to learn about her is with her own autobiography. St. Thérèse wrote her autobiography upon the instruction of her eldest sister, Mother Agnes, who was the Prioress at St.Thérèse's Carmel convent. It begins sweetly in Chapter1 with the following words: "My dearest mother, it is to you, to you who are in fact a mother twice over to me, that I now confide the story of my soul." See: St. Thérèse of Lisieux: "The Story of a Soul: the Autobiography of The Little Flower", published by Saint Benedict Press, 1990.

at the age of twenty-four. Her "Story of a Soul" is an inspiration for all readers to return to the simplicity and faith in God of a child, and the story of Thérèse's life would become a source of great inspiration for Mother Teresa. Before passing away, the final words that Thérèse whispered were: "My God, I love You."

Pope Pius X began the process to canonize Thérèse of Lisieux in 1914, and in 1925 she was canonized by one of his successors, Pope Pius XI. Pope Pius X had proclaimed her an unusually humble devotee to God. In 1997, as a testament to the value of her spiritual writing, Pope John Paul II gave Saint Thérèse of Lisieux the title of Doctor of the Catholic Church. She was only the 33rd person to receive this title in the Catholic Church's history, and the first woman to do so.

Mother Teresa was only eight years old when she heard and read about Saint Thérèse of Lisieux and about her wish to help people. Mother Teresa felt that she could do what Saint Thérèse had been forbidden to do, namely to go out and help the poor. This dream became a reality when Mother Teresa moved to Calcutta and began to help the neglected, the sick, and the destitute. Thus more than a century later, Saint Thérèse of Lisieux's legacy lives on today in the way she has inspired others to help the hungry and poor, and to lead a life of service to God. Pilgrims still flock to Normandy in northern France to visit the home where Saint Thérèse was born in the town of Alençon, and to pilgrimage sites in Lisieux. In the United States, the Carmelite Father Dolan founded the Society of the Little Flower in 1923 to teach people about the life and work of Saint Thérèse so that her "little way of spiritual childhood" could continue, and visitors come from afar to the beautiful National Shrine and Museum of St. Thérèse in Darien, Illinois.[9]

---

9 See: https://www.littleflower.org/learn-about/the-society-of-the-little-flower/, accessed on 5th November, 2019.

SAINT JOAN OF ARC

As we continued our stroll through the gardens of the Missionaries of Charity in Rome, Mother Teresa also mentioned Joan of Arc. I asked her why she was inspired by Joan of Arc. Mother Teresa went on to tell me how Joan of Arc was a poor girl who had received a calling from God and had answered that call, placing her faith completely in God. All her courage came from her love of God and her faith in God, and Mother Teresa found that inspiring.

Joan of Arc was born in France in the forest of Domremy on January 6, 1412.[10] She was the daughter of peasants and she could not read nor write; however, she was moved by her faith in God to undertake heroic acts that were unique for a woman of the early 15th century. At the age of 13, she had visions of the Archangel Michael and of saints, according to whom she was supposed to go and save France.

These were turbulent times: France was in the throes of the 100 years war with England. France had been losing ground in the war, Paris had been captured, along with Reims (where all French kings had been crowned for many centuries), and in 1429 Orléans was under siege – it was the last big city blocking access to the heart of France. Henry VI of England (as he would be known later) was close to victory over the future Charles VII of France (neither of them had been crowned king yet).

Joan of Arc proclaimed she was hearing God's words and that He had told her to protect France from foreign invaders and bring Charles VII to Reims for coronation. She went to the French garrison near her hometown to request an escort to Charles VII, but the officers believed

---

10 For a fascinating biography of the life of Joan of Arc, see Helen Castor: "Joan of Arc: A History", published by HarperCollins Publishers, New York, 2015. Other interesting versions include Allen Williamson's

"Biography of Joan of Arc", available at http://archive.joan-of-arc.org, accessed on 1st June, 2019.

she was insane. Nevertheless, as a result of a prediction she made, she was able to persuade them and, dressed in male clothing, she travelled across hostile territory to Charles VII's court in Chinon. She persuaded Charles VII that God had given her visions that she could lift the English siege of Orléans. Charles VII consulted with his advisors and, after she had been found by theologians at Poitiers to be of irreproachable morals, she was placed at the head of his army by the desperate Charles VII. Her victory at Orléans led to the siege being lifted within only nine days, and she came to be known as the Maid of Orléans.[11]

_____

11 The picture shows Joan of Arc on horseback, carrying her banner (she never carried weapons, seeking only to inspire French soldiers by encouraging them and placing herself in the same danger that they faced). Photo credit: Musée Dobrée, available at: https://commons.wikimedia.org/wiki/File:Joan of Arc on horseback.png, accessed on 1st June, 2019.

Her fighting spirit inspired Charles to retake Reims, and when he was crowned king, she was at his side. At that point, Joan wanted to return home because she felt her mission had been completed, but she was persuaded to remain. When the French army became less successful they held it against her, feeling her spirit was not the same when fighting. In a battle with the troops of Burgundy, who were allied with the English, Joan of Arc was taken prisoner and handed over to the English. She was tried for witchcraft and burned at the stake in Rouen on May 30, 1431.

Joan was of simple birth, but of strong character and deep spiritual beliefs. She became a French heroine, as the tide of the 100 years war turned definitively towards a French victory after the victory at Orléans. Joan's memory was vindicated by Pius X, who beatified her in 1909, and she was canonized by his successor, Benedict XV, in 1920.

Joan of Arc's legacy lives on and, five centuries later, she continues to inspire people. One of the people she inspired deeply is Mother Teresa, who admired Joan of Arc's strength and her devotion to God. Joan reminded Mother Teresa of her beloved father who fought for the rights of the people of Kosovo. Moreover, as Mother Teresa told me, reading about Joan of Arc made Mother Teresa feel stronger in fulfilling her own divine mission to help the poorest of the poor.

CHAPTER *IV*

MOTHER TERESA'S JOURNEY BEGINS

*"God has his own way in life, we must
never question Him."*

Mother Teresa

MOTHER TERESA'S EARLY YEARS

Anjezë Gonxha Bojaxhiu was born on August 26, 1910, as the youngest of three surviving children to Nikolië and Dranafile (nicknamed Drana) Bojaxhiu.[12] Her first name Anjezë is Albanian for Agnes, while her middle name, Gonxha, is Albanian for "bud" or "little flower". Agnes' older sister, Aga, was born in 1905, while her older brother Lazar was born in 1908. Agnes was baptized the day after she was born, and later in life she would use her baptism day, August 27, 1910, rather than her date of birth as her birthday.

Agnes' parents had met and married in a village called Peja, which is in

---

12 For excellent and complete biographies of the life of Mother Teresa, see: Kathryn Spink: "Mother Teresa (Revised and Updated): An Authorised Biography", published by HarperCollins, New York, 2011, and see: Jim Gallagher. "Mother Teresa", published by the Catholic Truth Society, available on https://issuu.com/catholictruthsociety/docs/b._mother_teresa, accessed on 7th May 2019.

what is today Albania, but left their hometown because of political upheaval and moved to Skopje, the capital of what is now the Republic of North Macedonia, which is where Agnes was born. The family lived a prosperous life in Agnes' early years, because Nicolië had a successful construction firm. However, Nicolië, who was active in politics and fought for Kosovar Albanian causes, fell sick and died suddenly after returning from a political gathering in Belgrade in 1919 (some have alleged he was poisoned). Thus Agnes lost her father when she was only nine years old.

Nicolië's death changed Agnes' family life forever. Nicolië's business partner in the construction firm took over the company and dispossessed Agnes' family of any assets in it. Drana sold much of what the family still had in order to gain an income, but she kept a nice house with a big orchard and vegetable garden in the back. In order to be able to provide for her children, and being very handy, Drana set up a small store after her husband's death where she sold lovely clothes and embroideries that she herself made. As a deeply religious woman, Drana raised her children in the Catholic faith and taught them how to pray. On Sundays she would take her children to the village church to attend Mass. Even though she did not have a lot, Drana would always invite poor people to her home to eat with her and her children. Her mother's devotion and charity made a strong impression on the young Agnes.

Agnes was an avid reader as a young girl and read books about Saint Francis, Saint Thérèse of Lisieux and Saint Joan of Arc. She was inspired by their devotion to God and how they had devoted themselves to helping other people. By the age of 12, Agnes had come to learn about missionaries and their work in West Bengal, India, thanks to conversations she had with Jesuit priests at her local church. The young Agnes was fascinated by the stories and began to yearn for a life of service to the poor.

She had also been on pilgrimage with her mother to the Shrine of the Black Madonna in Letnicë, which was in Kosovo, near the border with

Macedonia.

In August 1928, when Drana took her children on a pilgrimage to the Black Madonna, Agnes saw many sick people who had come to the Shrine to pray, wishing for a healing miracle. That day Agnes herself experienced a miracle: kneeling in front of the Black Madonna, Agnes had a vision and heard the voice of God, telling her that she was to go and help poor people.

MOTHER TERESA LEAVES HER HOME AND TRAVELS TO IRELAND

When she returned from her pilgrimage, Agnes discussed her ideas about helping poor people with her village priest, Father Jambrekovic. She had heard from a visiting Jesuit priest about the poor and sick in Calcutta, India, and about their struggle for survival under the worst conditions. She had listened carefully to the priest's words and then determined that she would one day go to Calcutta and help the poor, with God's help. After her experience at the Shrine in Letnicë, Agnes' mind was made up, even though Father Jambrekovic told her to take her time and finish her education before taking such a major step. One month later, after speaking at length with her mother, to whom she had become very attached after the death of her father, Agnes resolved to leave her home and begin her journey of lifetime service for the poor.

Agnes, her older sister Aga and their mother Drana, traveled to Zagreb, Croatia in September 1928. It is in Zagreb that Agnes bade farewell to her family. It was not easy for her to leave them, not knowing if she would ever see them again, and indeed she never saw her mother or sister alive again. Moreover, Agnes was concerned because she only spoke Albanian and Serbo-Croat at the time, (although she would later learn English, Hindi, Bengali and some French), but she placed her faith entirely in Jesus to guide her. Agnes boarded her train with Betike Kanje, whom she met in Zagreb and who also wanted to become a novice and missionary, and with whom she developed a strong friendship. They travelled together via Austria to Paris, France, where they were welcomed by Loreto Sisters and spent a couple of days at the Loreto House in Paris. After being interviewed by Sister Eugene, the Mother Superior, (with the help of an interpreter), Agnes and Betike travelled on to the Loreto Abbey in Rathfarnham, Ireland, where they arrived at the end of September 1928.

THE LORETO ABBEY IN RATHFARNHAM

In 1725, William Palliser had a luxurious mansion built on a large estate in Rathfarnham, on the south side of Dublin, Ireland. The Rathfarnham House was eventually purchased in 1821 by the Catholic Archbishop of Dublin, Dr. Daniel Murray, as a place to educate children. In 1822 Sister Frances Ball of the Sisters of Loreto, who was also known as Mother Teresa, established a school for girls at the Rathfarnham House and renamed it Loreto Abbey.

The Sisters of Loreto are formally known as the Institute of the Blessed Virgin Mary, I.B.V.M. Their congregation was founded in 1609 by Mary Ward, an Englishwoman who wanted to provide a good education for girls. The Sisters of Loreto got their name from a small town on the northeastern coast of Italy, close to Ancona. According to legend, the Blessed Virgin Mary is believed to have lived in Loreto and the Basilica of the Holy House was built over the site of her house in Loreto. Mary Ward used to pray at the basilica in Loreto and was inspired there to found the Sisters of Loreto. Today there are around 150 Loreto schools all around the world, including in Calcutta, India.

During our conversation on the flight from London to Rome, I asked

Mother Teresa about her time at the Loreto Abbey in Rathfarnham. She replied:

"Angela, arriving at the Loreto Abbey in Dublin really changed my life forever. When we arrived, the Mother Superior told Betike and me that it would not be easy to be a Sister of Loreto and, just like the Mother Superior in Paris, she asked us again whether we were really ready to devote our lives to Jesus. We were both ready to do so."

On 12th October, 1928, Sister Agnes became a Loreto postulant and chose to change her name to Sister Teresa. She said: "I chose the name Teresa for my religious vows. But it wasn't the name of the great Teresa of Avila. I chose the name of Teresa of the Little Flower. Thérèse of Lisieux."[13] Since there was already another Loreto Sister there with the name Thérèse, Mother Teresa chose to spell her name as "Teresa" instead of "Thérèse".

"I was happy at the Loreto Abbey, although I missed my family very much. Thankfully, Betike and I shared a room there. The house was impressive, like a big castle! Our days began at 6:00am. After attending Mass we would help to prepare breakfast. Then we would study. In the short time I was there, I had to learn how to write, read and speak English, and I had to study very hard to learn the language quickly! It was not easy! After our studies, I would either help in the Abbey or go out with the Loreto nuns to help the poor. In the evenings, before dinner, Betike and I would go to Mass again, and I prayed to God for His strength and support."

"Thank you for sharing this story with me, Mother Teresa." I said. "It sounds like you were happy there! Next time I am in Dublin I must visit the Loreto Abbey."

"Yes, at first it was difficult to be away from my home, but I had a happy time there. In fact, a few years ago I was able to go back to visit the

13 Quoted in Becky Benenate and Joseph Durepos, Editors. "Mother Teresa: No Greater Love", published by MJF Books, New York, 1997.

Loreto nuns at Rathfarnham. I had not been there in 46 years but had many happy memories when I went back."

"Mother Teresa, during your time at the Loreto Abbey, were you thinking ahead about your journey to Calcutta?" I wanted to know. Mother Teresa replied:

"Yes, that was on my mind the whole time! When we finally got permission to travel to India, I went to the chapel to thank God."

CHAPTER V

MOTHER TERESA TRAVELS TO CALCUTTA

"Keep the joy of loving the poor, and share the joy with all you meet, and God will bless you."

Mother Teresa

MOTHER TERESA'S JOURNEY TO CALCUTTA

The day finally came when Mother Teresa and her friend Betike left the Loreto Abbey in Rathfarnham to travel by sea to Calcutta, India. Mother Teresa told me about this part of her journey as we flew together from London to Rome.

"Angela, we were on the boat for many weeks before we reached Calcutta. I will never forget the trip. We passed through the Suez Canal, and from there we eventually reached the Bay of Bengal. Three Franciscan Sisters were travelling with us, so we would pray together every day. Betike and I would also listen to their stories about Calcutta, especially about the people living in incredible hunger and poverty.

"What was very sad for me while we were on the boat is that I spent my first Christmas there away from home and from my family and friends. Christmas at home was always so special, Angela. I would go to the church in our village with my mother and sister for Mass and we would pray in front of the beautiful Nativity. So I was very homesick that Christmas on the boat, but I prayed to God to give me strength, and He did.

"After some time we arrived at Port Said. We spent a few hours in town, and went to a church there for Mass. I had never before seen so many hungry people, begging for food. I felt terribly sad so I gave some of my food to a poor person, but I felt so helpless as so many other people staggered over to the person to whom I had given my food.

"I remember when we arrived in Colombo [Sri Lanka], we were met by Mr. Scalam, a brother who worked with the Loreto Sisters. He took us to the Loreto Sisters there, who were so nice and helpful to us. We were happy that we could understand them, having learnt some English in Dublin! Then a Jesuit priest joined us for the boat trip from Sri Lanka to India. He was going to India to preach about the life of Jesus. We joined him for Mass every day on the boat.

"Angela, on New Year's day we arrived in Madras. There I saw really deep poverty, the poorest of the poor, for the first time. The people were much poorer than in the other ports we had stopped in. I saw old and young people with hunger and deep despair in their eyes and babies with huge sad eyes and bony ribs. Angela, it broke my heart to see them, and I could not help crying. People were lying on the streets in the mud, dressed in rags and looking like skeletons, and stretching their hands out for us to give them food. Some were so weak that they could not even lift their hands to beg. All I could do was pray for them, as I did not even have any food to share. I promised God that in Calcutta I would go to help the children and the people as much as I could. It was a very moving and sad experience for me.

"Finally, in January, actually on Epiphany day, we arrived in Calcutta. We were taken straight to the Loreto Abbey. Again, there were so many hungry and desperately poor people around us that it broke my heart. As we drove to the Abbey, children ran barefoot alongside our car, knocking at the windows and begging with their small, outstretched hands. I looked at their sad, desperate eyes and my heart wept. I knew I needed to help them, but at that moment I felt overcome with sadness because I had nothing to give them. Later the Archbishop of Calcutta came and told us that our lives would change drastically and that we needed to devote ourselves to God and learn how to be real missionaries. Our lives did change forever, but we were ready to do God's work."

CHAPTER VI

MOTHER TERESA'S LIFE AND MISSION IN CALCUTTA

"I know God will not give me anything I can't handle,
I just wish that He didn't trust me so much."

Mother Teresa

MOTHER TERESA'S EARLY YEARS IN INDIA

We were in the airplane, flying from London to Rome, when Mother Teresa told me about her time in India. She began this part of her story by saying:

"Angela, I thanked God when we finally arrived in Calcutta. But as I stood on the railing of the ship I saw so many poor and hungry people waiting below that I thought that if the people at home saw this, they would never complain about their problems. When we got off the ship, my heart was so sad as I walked among their outstretched hands and saw their eyes filled with despair. Some of the children followed us, begging for food or money. You know, Angela, I asked God how I could help all the people. I said to Him: 'I need Your help. All I have is my two hands. Please help me, God.'"

Then Mother Teresa told me about the happier times she had in her early years in India as a teacher, but also about the difficult times around India's independence, and how she came to feel the need, or more accurately a calling from Jesus, to live among the poor to help them.

Mother Teresa was met on her arrival in Calcutta by the Sisters of Loreto, but after only a week in Calcutta, she travelled north to the Sisters of Loreto's house for novitiates in Darjeeling, which is in the Himalayas in the northern part of the Indian state of West Bengal. There she learned Hindi and Bengali and taught at the Sisters of Loreto's school. Two years later, on 24th May, 1931, she professed her vows of poverty, chastity and obedience as a Sister of Loreto.

After that, Mother Teresa was sent to Calcutta to teach catechism, as well as history and geography, at the Sisters of Loreto's school in Entally in Calcutta, but she ended up teaching at two other schools as well, including St. Mary's School, where she eventually became the headmistress.

"Mother Teresa, you must have been a wonderful teacher!" I said.

Mother Teresa smiled and answered modestly: "I don't know if I was a good teacher. You would have to ask the students! But I was very happy teaching at the schools in Entally. The girls I taught were very good. They loved to help the sick and the poor. You know, Angela, because of my vows, at that time I could not go to the slums or to the hospital with them to visit the sick and the poor, but later many of them joined the Missionaries of Charity to serve the poor."

Mother Teresa taught happily in Entally for many years, but every year she would return to Darjeeling for a spiritual retreat, and in 1937 she made her final profession of vows as a Sister of Loreto, affirming happily: "Now I am the spouse of Jesus for all eternity."[14]

---

14 See: https://motherteresa.org, accessed on 7th November, 2019.

"You know, Angela," Mother Teresa continued, as we talked on the flight to Rome. "Although I was very happy teaching, I was also saddened by the suffering of the poor I saw around me. There was so much hunger and sickness, and I could feel that so many of the poor had lost their hope. I wanted to help the poorest of the poor, I asked God for help and I made a vow to Jesus to do whatever he would ask me to do."

I held Mother Teresa's hand and said: "You know, Mother Teresa. I can imagine what you went through. When I was in Haiti, I saw so many poor and hungry people, living out in the open because they had no houses to sleep in. They used to build shelters with sticks to hold up banana leaves to shield them from the hot sun and the rain, but they would still get completely wet when it rained. I could not bear to see them suffering, and yet I did not know what to do. So I went out and got some little shirts for the naked babies and some tins of powdered milk as well as drinking water, and a huge plastic sheet that a few families could put over the top of their shelters to keep out the rain, as they had built their shelters close together. I remember how they smiled gratefully at me, and yet I still felt so helpless – I wished I could have done more for them. You must have felt the same in the slums in India, but you stayed there to help the people. Thank you!" I said, as I held Mother Teresa's hand, and she smiled sadly, lost for a moment in her thoughts.

The Second World War brought deep changes to Mother Teresa's life: the British army took over the Sisters of Loreto's facilities at Entally and the students had to be moved to other convents. A terrible famine in Bengal also led to hundreds of thousands of starving refugees pouring into Calcutta. After the war, violent conflicts broke out between Hindus and Muslims in 1946, while India's independence and its partition in 1947 into India and Pakistan led to more conflict and to countless thousands of poor refugees in Calcutta. It was during these troubled times, on 10th September 1946, that Mother Teresa had a mystical experience that changed her life. As we talked about these times, Mother Teresa looked me in the eyes and said: "Angela, I felt a call within a calling to serve Jesus."

Mother Teresa reflected for a moment and looked away before she turned back to me and continued: "I was on the train on my way to Darjeeling to recover, because I had fallen ill with tuberculosis, when Jesus told me I had to follow Him to the slums to help the poorest of the poor. When I felt His calling, I had no doubt about what I had to do; I just did not know how to do it, but I prayed to God for help and He guided me." After telling me this, Mother Teresa turned away for a moment to look out of the window of the plane and reflect in silence. I too reflected in silence about what she had just shared with me and about her immense devotion in answering the call of Jesus.

MOTHER TERESA ESTABLISHES HER MISSIONARIES OF CHARITY

When she had recovered from her bout of tuberculosis, Mother Teresa returned to Calcutta and reached out to her spiritual guide, Father Van Exem, and through him to Archbishop Ferdinand Perier of the Archdiocese in Calcutta so that she could be released from the restrictions of the Sisters of Loreto, who were cloistered and wore habits. She had contemplated on the calling she had received and knew that she had been called to form a new Order of sisters who would dress in simple Indian saris and live among and minister to the sick and dying in the slums of Calcutta. The Archbishop required Mother Teresa to wait one year to give full consideration to this petition, but during that year, Mother Teresa's conviction only grew stronger, and early in 1948, she got permission from the Archbishop and from the Mother Superior of the Sisters of Loreto in Ireland to be released from the restrictions of the Sisters of Loreto. However, a request for final permission for her to leave the cloistered life had to be sent to the Vatican in Rome.

On 17th August, 1948, with the permission of the Pope, Mother Teresa left the Convent of the Sisters of Loreto, where she had been so happy for almost twenty years, and changed her habit for a simple white cotton sari bordered with three blue stripes. It was the sari worn by the poor in Calcutta. The first thing she did was to go to live with the Medical Missionaries of Mary in Patna (in the Indian State of Bihar) for three months to learn all about providing basic medical care. Then in December that year, Mother Teresa returned to Calcutta to live with the Little Sisters of the Poor to begin to help the sick and the hungry on the streets and in the slums, who had been abandoned by their families and by society. On 21st December, 1948, Sister Mary Teresa went out to the slums of Mohil Jil for the first time to fulfill her 'call within the calling'.

"Mother Teresa," I asked. "Were you not frightened to walk alone through the streets in the slums?"

She held my hand and replied: "Yes, Angela, I must admit I felt a little frightened at first, more so during the day than at night. At night the poor would sleep, but during the day they would stare at me with deep suspicion. I would pray to myself and smile to them before walking on. Still, the first times I went into the slums I held on tightly to my Rosary and rested my hand on the crucifix that I wear on my left shoulder and I prayed to God and to Mary, the Mother of Jesus, to help me.

"When I began to teach the children in the slums I had no books and pens but I would sit on the ground with them and would write the alphabet and arithmetic on the earth with a stick. I would also teach them how special they were and how much God loved them. You know, Angela, when I began to teach the children and the parents saw that the children were laughing and were learning happily, the parents began to welcome me more."

In addition to teaching children, Mother Teresa began to minister to the sick and hungry. Mother Teresa told me: "I remember one of the first times I went out I saw a poor woman lying on the street, so I bent down and gave her some of my bread. She smiled at me and stroked my hand. I wished at the time that I had more bread to give her, but sometimes a small act of love can nourish a person's soul and I think that is what made her smile and reach out for my hand. Angela, there was so much suffering that I knew I could not help everyone, but I knew that, with God's help, I could at least try to help the person right in front of me."

I was overwhelmed as I listened to Mother Teresa recount her early work in the slums of Calcutta. I could not talk and just pressed her hand as tears rolled down my cheeks.

Two months later, in February 1949, Mother Teresa was blessed with support from a Catholic household, headed by Michael Gomes, who gave her a second-floor room free of charge to live in and from which to help the community. One month later, Subashini Das, one of Mother Teresa's former students from St. Mary's school joined her, and within a few months another nine former students had joined them. The Archbishop of Calcutta was pleased with the work done by Mother Teresa and her sisters and in 1950 he was able to persuade the Vatican to formally approve the establishment of the Order of the Missionaries of Charity, under the Archdiocese of Calcutta, with a vocation to serve the poorest.

"Angela, the work of our Missionaries of Charity is very simple.

We spend a part of our time helping those who are suffering and part of our time praying to God. We live simply, and we do not need much. Each Sister has two saris, a pair of sandals, a Rosary and a crucifix. "We are blessed to be able to serve those who have much less. Slowly things changed for us at the Missionaries of Charity. People began to come forward to us, bringing food, medical supplies and other contributions for the poor. That really helped. Whenever we needed something to help the poor, we prayed for God's help."

In 1952, after having worked for three years from Michael Gomes' home on 14 Creek Lane, the Missionaries of Charity were finally able to establish a home for the dying and destitute in Calcutta in a hostel next to a Hindu temple for the goddess Kali. "We named it Nirmal Hriday, which means 'Pure Heart'," Mother Teresa told me. "It was to be a place where the poorest of the poor, who were turned away by the medical system and even by their own families, could come to die with dignity and love."

Nirmal Hriday home for the dying and destitute[15]

"Angela, sometimes it is too late for us to be able to nurse people back to health," Mother Teresa continued. "The best we can do is to hold their hands and pray at their sides before they are called to God. We sometimes bring water from the Ganges for those who are Hindus, for Muslims we read to them from the Koran, and for Christians we pray with them to Jesus. But even if we cannot help them recover, being with them as they are called to God is also important, because people have a right to die with dignity. That can be as simple as knowing that there is someone at their side who cares about them and who gives them love in the final moments of their lives."

I had given little thought to this idea, as we rarely think about death, but Mother Teresa's words forced me to think about this. Death inspires us with so much fear that, as I listened to her and reflected on her words, I could understand why having loving support in the dying moments of one's life could be so important, and especially if a person had felt wretched and abandoned in his or her life up to that point.

One year later, in 1953, the Missionaries of Charity were able to establish their Motherhouse on 54 Lower Circular Road in Calcutta with support from Archbishop Perier of Calcutta, and the Motherhouse is still there today! Within the next few years, in addition to the Nirmal Hriday and the Motherhouse, the Missionaries of Charity had also established their first orphanage for children, called Nirmala Shishu Bhavan, as well as various schools and medical centers in Calcutta, mobile medical services (including to support lepers), and a home for lepers in Gobra, a suburb of Calcutta. After 1960, bishops in other states of India beyond West Bengal began to ask Mother Teresa to open centers in their dioceses as well, and the work of the Missionaries of Charity began to expand rapidly in India.

MOTHER TERESA'S WORK AND RECOGNITION EXPAND BEYOND INDIA

I looked at Mother Teresa, full of awe, as she spoke about her work and her dedication to the poor, and I was struck by how she had managed to inspire so many others to help the poor too. Mother Teresa told me about how the Sisters would cook the meals, do the washing and cleaning, tend to the sick and the orphans, manage the medical supplies, teach young children, or go with Mother Teresa to the slums to attend to and sometimes bring back pregnant women, sick babies and children, and adults in frail health to give them shelter, food, medicine and caring attention.

"Mother Teresa, how did you achieve it all?" I asked.

She took a deep breath and said: "With God's help and the help of our Sisters and Brothers and Co-workers. Each one of us must do our small part, but I could not have done it all alone. I also am able to do what I do only because of the love of Jesus. He is always there for us,

and even at those times when we cannot feel His presence, we must always have faith that He is there for us."

The recognition of the Missionaries of Charity expanded, first in India, where Mother Teresa was awarded the Order of the Lotus (Padma Sri) Prize by the IndianGovernment in 1962, and then beyond, when Pope Paul VI gave the Order of the Missionaries of Charity a global

approval that allowed them to work beyond India. In 1965, Mother Teresa and a few of her Sisters opened the first Missionaries of Charity house outside of India, in Venezuela. Other missions followed quickly in Europe (including Rome), Africa (beginning in Tanzania) and in Australia and the Americas.[16] Although Mother Teresa, being the humble person she was, shied away from media attention, she became famous after a BBC report on her by Malcolm Muggeridge and his subsequent book published in 1971.[17] She was invited to speak to large audiences around the world, and became more willing to spread the word not so much about her work or that of the Missionaries of Charity as about how every person is sacred and deserves dignity, and about the importance of every person loving their families and helping all who are poor, needy and abandoned. It is due to her invitation to a speaking engagement that I came to meet Mother Teresa for the third time, when we were both invited to attend the National Prayer Breakfast in Washington DC in February 1994, where she was the guest of honor (see below).

Mother Teresa and the Missionaries of Charity also received numerous awards, including some of the highest recognitions awarded by different countries and institutions, and in December 1979, Mother Teresa received the Nobel Peace Prize. The work of her Missionaries of Charity continued to spread around the globe, and by the time of her death in 1997, they were working in more than 120 countries.[18]

---

16 The picture of Mother Teresa on the previous page was taken at a meeting in Bonn, Germany, on the importance of life. Photo credit: TúrelioDerivative work: TharonXX [CC BY-SA 2.0 de (https://creativecommons.org/licenses/by-sa/2.0/de/deed.en)], available at: https://commons.wikimedia.org/wiki/File:MotherTeresa_094-1(cropped).jpg, accessed on 1st June, 2019.

17 Malcolm Muggeridge. "Something Beautiful for God: Mother Teresa of Calcutta", published by Harper & Row, Publishers, San Francisco, 1971.

18 See: https://motherteresa.org, accessed on 14th May, 2019.

MOTHER TERESA RECEIVED SUPPORT FROM MANY SPECIAL PEOPLE

The work of the Missionaries of Charity was supported by many people. Mother Teresa depended first and foremost on the selfless sacrifice and work of all the Sisters and Brothers of the Missionaries of Charity – at the time of her death there were more than 4,000 active and contemplative Sisters and Brothers all around the world – and of the countless co-workers who provided support. Mother Teresa also depended on donations from countless families, both rich and poor, and from businesses, other organizations, and the Church. And she was a tremendous fundraiser, working hard to persuade people to grant goods and services and financial resources to the Missionaries of Charity. No donation was too small for the work of the organization, as I witnessed in person when I saw Mother Teresa asked the flight attendants on our flight from London to Rome to donate the spare orange juices for her organization rather than dispose of them.

Mother Teresa also received guidance, moral support and solidarity from many key persons in the church, including: Fr. Van Exem, a Jesuit priest who provided spiritual guidance to Mother Teresa around the time of her calling within a calling, and who interceded on her behalf so she could receive approval for the Order of the Missionaries of Charity as well as for her to receive support for a home to work out of in Calcutta; Archbishop Perier of Calcutta, who took her petition for the establishment of the Order of the Missionaries of Charity to Rome, as well as several Indian bishops whose support contributed to Pope Paul VI's decision to grant the Order global validity; bishops in other parts of the world, who invited the Missionaries of Charity to help them in their dioceses; Archbishop Marcinkus, who frequently supported Mother Teresa as the head of the Vatican Bank; and Popes

Pius XII, John XXIII, Paul VI, John Paul I and, as we shall see later, Pope John Paul II.

One very special supporter of Mother Teresa was Jacqueline de Decker.[19] A Belgian by birth, Jacqueline traveled to India to do social work and met Mother Teresa late in 1947 while she was still in Patna, receiving training on nursing. Jacqueline and Mother Teresa shared a great devotion to God and to helping the poor and destitute, and Jacqueline wanted to join Mother Teresa in her work. Unfortunately Jacqueline became very sick and had to return to Belgium for a long series of operations on her spine.

Mother Teresa wrote to Jacqueline in 1952, saying: "Today I am going to propose something to you. You have been longing to be a missionary. Why not become spiritually bound to our society, which you love so dearly? While we work in the slums, you share in the prayers and the work with your suffering and your prayers. The work here is tremendous and needs workers, it is true, but I also need souls like yours to pray and suffer."[20] Thereafter, the two became so close spiritually that Mother Teresa would refer to Jacqueline as her "sick and suffering self", valuing Jacqueline's suffering as a contribution to her work, and in turn offering her work to God to support Jacqueline. Jacqueline was happy to know that she could still be of service by being connected spiritually with the work done for the sick and the poor.

Later, when I visited Mother Teresa at her Missionaries of Charity in Rome in 1981 and we had our second conversation, she told me: "Angela, remember that you can help too. Tell your members at the United Nations

---

19 See: Heather King. "Jacqueline de Decker", published by the Catholic Education Resource Center, available on https://www.catholiceducation.org/en/faith-and-character/faith-and-character/jacqueline-de-decker.html,

20 Quoted in ibid.

Women's Guild and all that you know about the poor and the hungry and the abandoned. If they can help that is good, but if they feel they cannot contribute, then their spiritual support and their suffering is also important for this work. Remember that many small acts of love, however small, can make a big change, but one must be patient and persistent to do so."

I could not help myself and took Mother Teresa's hand in mine and whispered: "Thank you for sharing all of this with me. I feel so humble." I felt Mother Teresa fingers curl around mine as she pressed my hand in friendship and smiled.

CHAPTER VII

THE INAUGURATION OF MOTHER TERESA'S FRIEND
POPE JOHN PAUL II

"Faith and reason are like two wings of the human spirit
by which it soars to the truth."

Pope John Paul II

POPE JOHN PAUL II'S INAUGURATION IN ST. PETER'S SQUARE

It was 16th October 1978. I was standing in St. Peter's Square, near the entrance to the Vatican (or St. Peter's Basilica, as it is known). The cardinals were gathered for the third day in a Papal Conclave to elect a new pope, following the death of Pope John Paul I on 28th September 1978 after only 33 days as Head of the Catholic Church. With every unsuccessful vote, in which no candidate received the required votes, black smoke had poured out of the chimney over the Sistine Chapel. Then suddenly it was there: white smoke billowed out of the chimney, and the crowds in the Piazza (square) began to shout joyfully in Italian: *"Abbiamo un nuovo papa!"* which translates as: "We have a new pope!" The cardinals had chosen Cardinal Karol Wojtyla, the first non-Italian to be chosen to lead the Catholic Church in more than 450 years, to be the new Pope.

I remember the excitement as we looked up and saw the newly elected Pope step out onto the balcony of the Vatican overlooking St. Peter's Square. The balcony had been decorated quickly for the occasion with a dark red rug hanging down from it, covered in turn by a white flag bearing the papal coat of arms. Instead of addressing us in English or Latin or in his native Polish, the newly elected Pope endeared himself to the crowd gathered in the square below him by speaking to them in Italian, saying: "Dear brothers and sisters, we are saddened at the death of our beloved Pope John Paul I, and so the cardinals have called for a new Bishop of Rome. They called him from a faraway land—far and yet always close because of our communion in faith and Christian traditions. I was afraid to accept that responsibility, yet I do so in a spirit of obedience to the Lord and total faithfulness to Mary, our most Holy Mother."[21]

October 22, 1978 was a very special day. That day, Cardinal Karol Wojtyla was inaugurated as Pope John Paul II in a beautiful ceremony at the Vatican. I was there to witness this special occasion. How can I ever fully describe the inauguration celebration that I had the privilege to attend? The best I can perhaps do is to give a flavor of this moving occasion.

At the front of St. Peter's Square, a large altar had been set up, covered with embroidered, snow-white linen, and lined on the front with beautiful flowers. A tall, engraved,

21 Photo credit: This picture of Pope John Paul II dates back to 1993, when he visited the United States. It is available at: https://commons.wikimedia.org/wiki/File:JohannesPaul2-portrait.jpg, accessed on 1st June, 2019.

bronze cross stood on one side of the altar and a bible rested on the altar on a hand-carved bookstand.

Over 50 cardinals clad in gold and white embroidered robes and wearing their red *zucchetto* skullcaps or tall conical mitres lined the front row on either side of the altar. More cardinals, as well as archbishops and other senior clergy were seated behind them in several rows on the left side of the altar as you face the Vatican. The cardinals wore dazzling red robes, while other senior clergy wore black and/or white frocks. On the right side of the altar as you face the Vatican, behind the front row of cardinals, sat several rows of dignitaries and special guests for the inauguration. To the front of the altar, a series of steps led down to the main area of the square, which was brimming with countless thousands of pilgrims from all around the world, while photographers and others had taken prized positions at the top of Bernini's famous colonnades that surround St. Peter's Square to take photographs of the historic occasion.

In the front row of dignitaries and special guests, I could see King Juan Carlos and Queen Sophia of Spain. The Queen wore a beautiful white robe and her Spanish Mantilla. Next to them sat King Baudouin and Queen Fabiola of Belgium, who was dressed completely in black, as well as Prince Rainier and Princess Grace of Monaco, among other royalty and Heads of State. Distinguished guests of the diplomatic corps accredited to the Vatican, as well as senior officials of the Republic of Italy sat behind them.

My husband, Dr. McDonald Benjamin, and I attended the inauguration on behalf of the International Fund for Agricultural Development (IFAD) of the United Nations. We were seated a few rows behind the King and Queen of Spain. As I looked out upon the magnificent crowd, I could feel the excitement in the air. One could see the hope and expectations in people's faces and the air resonated with the emotions carried by their voices across St. Peter's Square (please see the photograph below that I took that day of the crowds as they eagerly awaited the Inauguration of Pope John Paul II).[22]

I felt humbled to be there on that historic day. As I lived in Rome, I had been to the Vatican many times. I had walked through the Holy Door, which was to my right, behind me, and which was opened only in Jubilee years (i.e. every twenty-five years) or on very special occasions. I had walked up the nave inside St. Peter's Basilica, lined with massive columns. I had stood before Michelangelo's marble masterpiece known as *La Pietá*, in which Mother Mary wistfully embraces her son Jesus after his death on the cross, and I had stroked the foot of the bronze statue of St. Peter near the altar, with its toes worn away by the touch

22 I took this photograph of the huge crowd attending Pope John Paul II's Inauguration from where my husband, Ambassador McDonald Benjamin, and I were seated.

of countless faithful hoping for the saint's blessing. I had stood before the altar and looked up at Bernini's famous dome towering above it. I had walked down the steps near the altar to the catacombs below, where many of the earlier popes are buried. And I had looked out through the main doors of the Vatican onto St. Peter's Square, embraced by its four rows of massive columns, built by Bernini more than 300 years earlier to suggest the embrace of Mother Church. And yet this day was unique.

Suddenly the air was filled with even greater excitement and cheers went up when Pope John Paul II and his entourage came out of St. Peter's Basilica through those very same doors, and walked slowly to the altar outside. Standing there, he looked up for a moment and then blessed us all. In the course of a moving ceremony, Pope John Paul II held a Mass and gave his first homily as pope, speaking in more than 10 languages to the faithful in St. Peter's Square and to the millions more watching on television. He reminded us how St. Peter had been called to Rome by God, and he spoke of his own unworthiness, and asked us to pray for him so that he might be able to serve. Afterwards, the cardinals stepped forward to kiss the pope's ring and commit their support to the new pope, before John Paul II blessed the crowd again and went inside, carried by the cheers and the applause of a deeply moved crowd. It was a beautiful and moving ceremony, one that I shall never forget.

MEETING THE NEW POPE AT HIS INAUGURAL RECEPTION

My husband and I were invited not only to attend the inauguration, but also to join the new Pontiff at a special reception at the Vatican later that evening. When we arrived at the Vatican, we were guided to the reception by a priest.

Suddenly I found myself only three feet away from the pope! He was standing near a door with a clergyman who I guessed was his personal secretary, Stanislaw Dziwisz. Seeing the pope standing so close by, my nerves overcame me and my heart started to beat like the drums of the Caribbean!

A moment later, the pope turned towards me and looked at me. My throat was dry, but with a crackly voice I managed to say: "Your Holiness, I am deeply blessed and honored to be here to share this most wonderful occasion with you. May God always be at your side."

The pope looked at me with his sincere blue eyes and answered: "Thank you my child, and may God be with you too." When he looked at me I felt as if he were searching deep within me, to my soul. I felt humble and full of gratitude to God. I felt so special! I could not comprehend what was happening to me, and whispered my deep gratitude to God.

The pope's personal secretary then asked all the guests to kindly follow the pope. We all followed the pope to the end of a wide corridor, where a priest stood and held open another door and we found ourselves inside the Sistine Chapel! I had never seen the Sistine Chapel before like this, and under my breath I whispered to myself: "How incredibly beautiful!"

The Sistine Chapel was lit by floodlight! The light was so bright that it brought all the paintings alive. It was as if the characters were stepping out of the paintings tobe with us. The colors of ancient times, cobalt blue, crimson red, sunflower yellow and emerald green, beamed magnificently from the walls of the sacred chapel. Looking at Michelangelo's "Last Judgment" illuminated in this way, I could not find words to describe my feelings. It just took my voice away. I just stared and then I found that many of the other guests were equally awestruck. And when I looked up at Michelangelo's painting at the center of the chapel's ceiling, where Adam was stretching towards God to receive his blessing, with their fingers almost touching, I knew I was the one who was touched in my heart. I felt God was blessing me in that moment. And I joined the many guests who were turning to the pope and simply saying to him: "Thank you, your Holiness, thank you!"[23]

Up to this day I will never forget those special moments in the Sistine Chapel, and the pope being with us and sharing this unique moment with us. A bishop, who was standing near me and watching me admire the Sistine Chapel in this light, told me that the Sistine Chapel is only illuminated by floodlights on the most special occasions, as the bright light would otherwise destroy the colors.

We were not the only ones to be blessed by the pope's warm presence that evening. Later, our chauffeur told us that he too received a special treat: Pope John Paul II had stepped outside and gone from car to car, shaking hands with and thanking each chauffeur personally for bringing his guests to him. I can only imagine the thrill that each of the chauffeurs must have felt that evening.

---

23 Photo credit: Image by Michael Scale on Pixabay. Available at: https://pixabay.com/illustrations/the-creation-of-adam-michelangelo-4889767/ Accessed on 13th October, 2022.

What a wonderful treat! We all felt so special. This evening silently spoke, loud and clear, about the humble and kind person Pope John Paul II would be as pope: the people's pope.

CHAPTER VIII

MOTHER TERESA'S SPECIAL FRIENDSHIP WITH
POPE JOHN PAUL II

"Don't be afraid to take a chance at peace, to teach peace, to live peace. Peace will be the last word of history."

Pope John Paul II

"The fruit of prayer is the deepening of faith, and the fruit of faith is love, and the fruit of love is service, and the fruit of service is peace."

Mother Teresa

TWO HISTORIC FIGURES DEVOTED TO COMPASSIONATE SERVICE

The friendship of Pope John Paul II and of Mother Teresa is a remarkable one. Both worked tirelessly and in unprecedented ways to bring messages of peace and love around the world. During his 26-year papacy, the third longest in history, John Paul II made 104 visits to foreign countries, more than all previous popes combined, travelling over 725,000 miles to visit 129 countries. The pope also made 145 trips and visited thousands of parishes inside Italy. When he held a mass in Ireland in September 1979, one-third of the country attended the mass, and when around 5,000,000 people gathered to see Pope John Paul II in Mexico in 1979 and a similar number came together to see him later in the Philippines, these meetings are believed to have been the largest human gatherings in history.

Pope John Paul II also played an immense role in advancing peace at a global level: his messages of apologies for past wrongs perpetrated by Catholics, especially against Jews and Muslims, opened spaces for reconciliation. For example, in 2000 he made a historic visit to the Holy Land and in 2001 he became the first Pope to enter a mosque to pray (in Damascus, Syria). Moreover, Pope John Paul II's 1979 pilgrimage to the Lady of Fatima in Poland played an inspirational role in the transformation of his home country by the Solidarity movement in the 1980s, which in turn contributed to the fall of the Iron Curtain and the end of the Cold War.

While Pope John Paul II inspired people at a global level with his messages of peace and reconciliation, Mother Teresa spread messages of peace, hope and love at a community level among the most impoverished and forsaken people around the world. At the time of her passing in 1997, Mother Teresa's Missionaries of Charity had over 3,800 sisters serving the poor and the suffering in almost 600 houses in 120 countries, as well as almost 400 fathers and brothers in more than 70 houses serving in more than 20 countries.[24]

The friendship and collaboration of these two magnificent persons and their presence in the world serving at the same time are gifts from God.

---

24 Mother Teresa's inspiring mission only continued to grow after her passing: by 2015, there were more than 5,000 sisters serving in more than 750 houses in 139 countries. See: https://motherteresa. org, accessed on 27th March, 2019.

FROM KAROL WOJTYLA TO POPE JOHN PAUL II

Born in the small town of Wadowice, Poland in 1920, Karol was raised in a humble apartment next to the town church.[25] After Karol lost his mother Emilia and his older brother Edmund at a young age, Karol's father, who was a military man, turned ever closer to the church, and inspired the young Karol to do the same. Karol, who was an excellent student at school, also loved playing football, acting, skiing and hiking in the mountains. His quiet life changed dramatically with the Nazi invasion in 1939. In order to avoid arrest, he worked at a factory, even as he wrote plays for a resistance theater called the Rhapsodic Theater. After his father died in 1941, Karol decided to join the church and soon began to attend illegal seminary classes, before being ordained as a priest in 1946. By that time the World War, with all the horrors that Karol had witnessed, was over, but still the Church was seen with suspicion and was repressed by the new Communist rulers in Poland.

As a young man, Karol had tremendous courage but also an endearing humility about him: once, when nuns saw that he had gone out poorly clothed into the winter cold, nuns knitted a sweater for him. Karol thanked them for the gift and promptly gave it to a poor fellow who was also suffering from the cold. When he was told that he had holes in his shoes, Karol joked that his feet would get nice cool air, and carried on wearing the shoes until they finally gave way!

---

25 There are a number of good biographies of the life of Pope John Paul II. As an example, see George Weigel: "Witness to Hope: The Biography of Pope John Paul II", published by HarperCollins Publishers, 1999. For a briefer summary of the Pope's life, see the: "Biographical Profile of Pope John Paul II (1920-2005)", available at http://www.vatican.va/special/canonizzazione-27042014/documents/biografia_gpii_canonizzazione_en.html, accessed on 3rd June, 2019.

Karol completed a doctorate in Rome in 1948 and returned to Poland, where he became a dynamic parish priest, a prolific writer, and a continuing student, completing a second doctorate by 1958. That year, he was appointed Bishop of Krakow and after gaining recognition for his interventions during the second Vatican Council in Rome during 1958-63, Karol was appointed Archbishop of Krakow in 1963 and Cardinal in 1967. Karol often bravely defied the Communist authorities in Poland, holding open air masses, speaking to large gatherings and even gaining permission to build a new church in 1977.

When Pope Paul VI died in 1978, the humble Albino Luciani from Venice was elected pope. He took the name John Paul I, in honor of Popes John XXIII and Paul VI, who had preceded him and who had overseen the second Vatican Council. Pope John XXIII in particular had hoped that the Council would promote the modernization of the church, although stiff resistance from more conservative parts of the Roman Curia (or church administration) and John XXIII's failing health meant he could not see this through. This mission did, however, inspire John Paul I, who never expected to be elected pope (and simply shrugged his shoulders when he first stepped out onto the balcony of the Vatican on 26th August, 1978 to greet the faithful in St. Peter's Square). He was the first pope to refuse to be crowned, and he also did not want to use the *gestatorial chair* (a throne-like chair on which the popes were carried above the crowds).

Pope John Paul I came in with the intention to promote reforms in the church, which at the time was mired in rumors of scandals, including the alleged participation of leading church figures in a masonic lodge (an excommunicable offence) and alleged linkages between the Vatican Bank and the mafia. However, Pope John Paul I died after only 33 days as pope, giving rise to conspiracy theories about the circumstances of his death. Cardinal Karol Wojtyla was then elected pope by the Conclave as he was seen as a good compromise between reformists and conservatives, and a younger person who could energize the faithful, especially youth. I was in St. Peter's Square on 16th October, 1978, when white smoke finally emerged from the chimney over the Sistine Chapel and the jubilant crowd began to cry out: "*Abbiamo un nuovo papa!*" ("We have a new pope!"). In honor of his predecessors, and also to signal his intent to continue reforming the church, Cardinal Wojtyla took on the name of John Paul II. Pope John Paul II began an active papacy, marked by unprecedented travel around Italy and around the world to promote his messages of Christian fellowship and values, but also of human rights, rejection of materialism and of repression, and respect for people. His mission almost came to a tragic end on 13th May 1981, when a Turkish assailant, Mehmet Ali Ağca, fired several shots at the pope in St. Peter's Square as he greeted the faithful from his Popemobile. Two bullets struck the pope in the abdomen and close to the heart. The pope was taken immediately to the Gemelli hospital and, after a five-hour surgery and large blood transfusions due to his significant loss of blood, they were able to save the pope's life.

After 64 days, the pope was allowed to leave the hospital to return to the Vatican. Since the assassination attempt happened on the feast of Our Lady of Fátima, the pope would later say that, Mary, the Mother of Jesus, had saved him, as she had done on previous occasions when he had faced threats earlier in his life. Later, the pope travelled to the Shrine of Our Lady of Fátima and laid the *zucchetto* he was wearing on the day of the assassination attempt at her feet and placed one of the bullets that struck him on the crown of the statue of Our Lady of Fátima. He also placed the blood-stained and bullet-pocked belt of his cassock at the Jasna Gora shrine in Czestochowa, Poland, in homage to the Virgin Mary, who he believed interceded on his behalf to save his life. Pope John Paul II was deeply devoted to the Virgin Mary, and throughout his papacy he would use the prayer "*Totus Tuus*" (which is Latin for "Totally Yours"), to express his complete devotion to the Virgin Mary, as can be seen in the message I received from Pope John Paul II (below) on the occasion of the 25th (Jubilee) Anniversary of his papacy.[26]

Later, on the 25th anniversary of his shooting, Pope Benedict XVI would announce the placement of a marble slab in St. Peter's Square to mark the exact spot at which Pope John Paul II was shot.

---

26 This beautiful handwritten note from Pope John Paul II commemorates the 25th Anniversary of his Papacy (from 16th October 1978 to 16th October 2003), and once again shows his devotion to the Virgin Mary with his prayer of "*Totus Tuus*" (i.e. "Totally Yours").

Pope John Paul II also took the extraordinary step of visiting his assailant in prison in 1983 and forgiving him personally. Unconfirmed allegations have suggested that the Soviet Union, working through the Bulgarian secret service, might have been behind Mehmet Ali Ağca's assassination attempt, because of the threat the Soviets felt from Pope John Paul II's messages to the faithful in Eastern Europe. What is certain is that this event did not prevent the pope from continuing to advocate for religious freedom and human rights.

MOTHER TERESA'S FRIENDSHIP WITH POPE JOHN PAUL II

The attack on Pope John Paul II in May 1981 happened not too long after I had met Mother Teresa for the second time in Rome, in the spring of 1981. On that occasion, as we walked through the garden of her Missionaries of Charity in Rome, Mother Teresa shared with me some of her thoughts about her friend Pope John Paul II, saying:

"Tomorrow I am meeting with the pope. He is a pope of very few words, but is a fine listener. He sent me an airplane ticket and asked me to come and see him. You know, Angela, the pope is building up the church and I am, with God's grace, building missions for the poor. In life nothing is easy, but if you believe in God, it makes it much easier. That is why we must always pray. If we want to grow personally and come closer to God, we must pray to Him, and humbly accept with a grateful heart everything that we receive and every opportunity that we are given to help others."

As she spoke to me about Pope John Paul II, her face lit up with a smile and an unbelievable brightness in her eyes that spoke louder than words about her sincere appreciation and respect for the pope and his work. Her voice sounded soft and yet resonant at the same time, and her face radiated with a special kind of transparency and brightness that is hard to explain. This respect and appreciation was mutual: Pope John Paul II would often invite Mother Teresa to visit him in Rome, and during her visits they would pray together in his personal chapel. As we shall see below, Pope John Paul II went to Calcutta to see Mother Teresa's work there in person, and when Mother Teresa passed away, Pope John Paul II waived the traditional waiting period to begin the process of canonizing her as a Saint. It was clear to me from the way that Mother Teresa spoke about her friendship with and respect for Pope John Paul II, that these two dear friends were destined to work together, each in their own way, for peace and compassion in the world.[27]

27 This picture, taken on 20th May 1997, reflects the beautiful friendship between Pope John Paul II and Mother Teresa. Photo credit: L'Osservatore Romano / FILE Pool Photo, reprinted with permission of the Associated Press.

Indeed, one way in which they worked together was to help the homeless in Rome. On a subsequent visit to Rome in 1987, Pope John Paul II took Mother Teresa out onto his balcony at the Vatican overlooking St. Peter's Square and pointed to the homeless people seeking shelter below under Bernini's colonnades. He asked Mother Teresa to build a shelter for them and, with help from the Vatican, one year later her Missionaries of Charity established a shelter and food distribution center for the homeless inside the Vatican City.

POPE JOHN PAUL II VISITS MOTHER TERESA IN CALCUTTA

One year earlier, in February 1986, Mother Teresa had celebrated what she later called "The happiest day of my life." Pope John Paul II's first stop in his visit to Calcutta, India, was at the Nirmal Hriday ashram that Mother Teresa had established as a hospice for the dying and suffering. When Pope John Paul II arrived in his 'Popemobile', Mother Teresa boarded the vehicle and bent down to kiss the pope's ring, and he in turn kissed her forehead. She then led the pope, holding him by the hand and guided him through the ashram. The pope greeted and blessed the people living in the ashram, took some of them into his arms in warm embraces, helped the nuns feed the sick, and blessed the corpses of some patients who had died. He was deeply moved by this experience.

When he left the ashram, the pope briefly addressed the crowd outside, referring to Nirmal Hriday as "a place that bears witness to the primacy of love." The pope went on to say: "Nirmal Hriday proclaims the profound dignity of every human person. The loving care which is shown here bears witness to the truth that the worth of a human being is not measured by usefulness or talents, by health or sickness, by age or creed or race. Our human dignity comes from God our Creator, in whose image we are all made. No amount of privation or suffering can ever remove this dignity, for we are always precious in the eyes of God."[28]

Mother Teresa said of her friend Pope John Paul II's visit that: "It is a wonderful thing for the people, for his touch is the touch of Christ." She was truly touched by his visit to the ashram, for it had indeed been the happiest day of her life.

TWO DEAR FRIENDS BECOME SAINTS

The friendship of these two special people with a mission of service would continue for more than a decade, before God called Mother Teresa to Him in 1997. After her death, Pope John Paul II waived the five-year waiting period that is traditionally observed and the Holy See began the process for canonization. When Mother Teresa was beatified in 2003, Pope John Paul II said: "Let us praise the Lord for this diminutive woman in love with God, a humble Gospel messenger and a tireless benefactor of humanity. In her we honor one of the most important figures of our time. Let us welcome her message and follow her example."[29] Mother Teresa was later declared a saint in September 2016 at a ceremony in St. Peter's Square led by Pope Francis that was attended by tens of thousands of faithful.

---

28 See: "The beautiful meeting of John Paul II and Mother Teresa", written by Mary Rezac for Catholic Online, accessed at https://www.catholic.org/news/hf/faith/story.php?id=71527 on 27th March, 2019. Also see quotations by Pope John Paul II in "Love is the Explanation of Everything: 365 Meditations with the Pope", published by Rizzoli International Publications, New York, 2011.

29 Quoted in Libreria Editrice Vaticana. "Beatification of Mother Teresa of Calcutta: Homily of His Holiness John Paul II, https://www.vatican.va/content/john-paul-ii/en/homilies/2003/documents/hf_jp-ii_hom_20031019_mother-theresa.html, 2003. Accessed on 2nd May, 2019."

Pope John Paul II passed away eight years after Mother Teresa, in April 2005. His loyal friend and secretary, Archbishop Stanislaw Dziwisz, was at the pope's side in his dying moments. Indeed, Archbishop Dziwisz reportedly opened the windows of the papal apartments so that the pope could hear Polish youths standing below who were singing sad Polish ballads and praying for the pope. His funeral on 8th April, 2005 led to the largest gathering of Heads of State in history outside of the United Nations.

Pope John Paul II was succeeded by Pope Benedict XVI, who also waived the traditional five-year waiting period and launched the process for beatification and canonization of Pope John Paul II in May 2005. Pope John Paul II was beatified in 2011 and, in a ceremony at the Vatican led by Pope Francis in April 2014, Pope John Paul II was canonized, together with Pope John XXIII. The canonization of John Paul II was one of the fastest on record.

Thus it is that the two dear friends, who had led lives of courageous and selfless service, came to be recognized as saints for the inspirational lives that they had led.

CHAPTER IX

MEETING ANOTHER FRIEND OF MOTHER TERESA:
ARCHBISHOP MARCINKUS

*"I used to believe that prayer changes things, but now
I know that prayer changes us and we change things."*

Mother Teresa

GOD'S BANKER

Among Mother Teresa's closer friends was Archbishop Paul Casimir Marcinkus, the Head of the Vatican Bank (or *Instituto per le Opere di Religione,* as it is formally known).[30] Born in Cicero, Illinois in 1922, Marcinkus was the fourth child of Lithuanian immigrant parents. After completing his studies at Catholic seminaries, Markincus was ordained as a priest in 1947 and served in Chicago's South Side. In 1950 he matriculated at the Gregorian University in Rome,

---

30 Photo credit: this picture of Archbishop Paul Marcinkus was originally published by www.repubblica.it. It is available at https://commons.wikimedia.org/wiki/File:Paul_Casimir_Marcinkus.jpg accessed on 1st June 2019.

where he befriended Giovanni Battista Montini (who would later become Pope Paul VI). After earning his degree in 1953, Marcinkus was
posted in Bolivia and Canada before returning to Rome in 1959 to
work at the Vatican's Secretariat of State.

At six foot three inches tall, and as an informal bodyguard
for Pope Paul VI, Marcinkus came to be known as "the Gorilla"!
Indeed, Marcinkus' prowess and attentiveness saved Pope Paul VI's
life, as he averted a knife attack on the pope during the pontiff's trip to
the Philippines in 1970. Marcinkus was highly devoted to protecting
the pope: a year earlier, he had prevented US Secret Service officers
from attending a private meeting between the pontiff and US President Richard Nixon, telling them: "I'll give you 60 seconds to get out
of here or you can explain to the president why the pope could not see
him today."[31]

Pope Paul VI greatly appreciated Markincus' organizational skills
and his language skills as an interpreter (Markincus spoke English,
French, Spanish, Italian and his native Lithuanian), and soon put him
in charge of organizing his foreign trips, and as the pope's confidence
in Marcinkus grew further, he was raised to Titular Archbishop of
Orta, and soon he became the highest-ranking American ever to serve
in the Vatican. In particular, in 1971, Archbishop Marcinkus, who had
joked that: "My only previous financial experience was handling the
Sunday collection!" was appointed Head of the Vatican Bank. A
year later, Archbishop Markinkus was appointed President of the
Roman Curia, and nine years later, under Pope John Paul II, appointed-
Pro-President of the Pontifical Commission for the Vatican City State,

---

31 This informal bodyguard role continued with Pope John Paul II, and indeed in 1982, Marcinkus also
saved Pope John Paul II's life, this time by preventing an assassination attempt on the Pope by a mad priest
during the Pope's visit to Our Lady of Fátima in Portugal.

before resigning in 1990.[32] After his resignation, and with the full support of Pope John Paul II, Archbishop Marcinkus returned to the United States, first to Chicago and then to Sun City, Arizona, where he served as a parish priest until his death in 2006 (one year after his dear friend John Paul II had passed away).

Archbishop Marcinkus' tenure as Head of the Vatican Bank was unfortunately overshadowed by allegations of improprieties relating to alleged financial dealings with persons associated with a masonic lodge and with the mafia, and for many years Italian prosecutors sought to question and even arrest the archbishop, until an Italian court ruled that they did not have jurisdiction over him. Archbishop Marcinkus always declared himself innocent of all the charges and hoped that, with time, he would come to be exonerated.

At Archbishop Marcinkus' funeral, Bishop Robert Lynch, who delivered the eulogy, recalled the pain and loneliness that Archbishop Marcinkus felt in his later years in Rome as a result of the allegations, stating that: "Throughout the difficult moments of his final years in Rome, the Archbishop hoped in silence, trusted in the truth one day to be revealed, and waited for and sought the Lord. He knew the great apostle Paul's words to the Romans: 'Hope does not disappoint.'… There is a part of me that would like to initiate the process of exoneration of his name, but this is not the place or the occasion…but I pray this will happen."[33]

In his eulogy, Bishop Lynch also recalled at length Archbishop Marcinkus' innumerable acts of kindness and his great sense of humor. Indeed, this extremely kind, funny, dependable, straight-speaking,

---

32 See http://www.catholic-hierarchy.org/bishop/bmarcp.html, accessed on 29th March, 2019.

33 See "A final farewell for God's Banker'" by Margaret Ramirez, at: https://www.chicagotribune.com/news/ct-xpm-2006-03-03-0603030276-story.html, accessed on 29th March, 2019.

generous and caring gentle giant is the Archbishop Marcinkus that I got to know, thanks to our friendship and to my friendship with Mother Teresa.

MY FIRST MEETING WITH ARCHBISHOP MARCINKUS

When I met Mother Teresa for the second time in 1981 at her Missionaries of Charity in Rome, she told me that she would introduce me to Archbishop Paul Marcinkus, the Head of the Vatican Bank. She kept her promise to me: Before I left her that day, she gave me Archbishop Marcinkus' private telephone number and asked me to pay him a courtesy call, and when I called shortly after that, I found that she had spoken to the archbishop about me and that he was expecting my visit.

The day of the visit, my son McDonald Jr. and I drove to the Vatican to meet with Archbishop Marcinkus at his office. We approached the Vatican City from the Viale R. Angelico and, after the Swiss Guards had checked our IDs and confirmed with Archbishop Marcinkus' office, we were guided to his office at the Vatican Bank, which is in the Sixtus V Courtyard of the Vatican City.

Following the instructions of the Swiss Guards, we drove through a short tunnel to a parking lot, where a priest was waiting for us to accompany us up to Archbishop Marcinkus' office. After stepping out of the elevator, we walked towards his office along a magnificent corridor with a beautiful Carrera marble floor, priceless tapestries and paintings by famous artists.

My heart was beating with excitement as we entered the archbishop's office. He stood up and gave us a warm welcome. He looked very impressive in his black cassock with a red trim and red buttons. Around his neck he wore a beautiful golden chain with a cross. I bent and kissed his ring (as a Catholic sign of respect) and then looked up at his towering 6 foot 3 inch frame. I could not help myself and spontaneously said: "Good Lord, you are tall!" He laughed, and I quickly felt at ease. I introduced my son McDonald Jr. and then presented myself as the President of the United Nations Women's Guild in Rome.

Archbishop Marcinkus' office looked impressive. On his fine, dark wooden desk there were telephones, a leather-bound Bible and expensive-looking writing materials. The floor of the office was covered with plush oriental carpets and a painting of Pope John Paul II hung on one wall. The office looked richly decorated, yet one had a feeling of natural warmth in it. As we sat in front of Archbishop Marcinkus' desk, he sat back in his leather-framed chair behind the desk and looked so relaxed that I felt as if he had all the time in the world for us, even though I knew that he had numerous responsibilities as the President of the Vatican Bank and the newly appointed Head of the Pontifical Commission for the Vatican City, not to mention as organizer of papal trips and unofficial personal bodyguard of the pope. With a big smile, Archbishop Marcinkus then looked at me and asked: "So, what can I do for you?"

"Monsignor," I answered. "I am very grateful to you for finding the time to meet with me today. Mother Teresa was very eager for me to meet with you. This is a courtesy call as President of the United Nations Women's Guild in Rome, but I would also like to discuss a financial matter with you, since the UNWG would like to support Mother Teresa's Missionaries of Charity and I understand that this might be possible via the Vatican Bank as the Missionaries of Charity have accounts at the Vatican Bank. Is that correct?"

Archbishop Marcinkus confirmed this with a smile, and then asked me to tell him more about the about the work of the United Nations

Women's Guild. I told him about the many ways in which we had been able to support children around the world through a wide range of projects, such as cataract operations to restore eyesight to blind children in Bangladesh; artificial skin replacements for indigenous children in Brazil who had suffered terrible burns; wells to improve access to safe drinking water in Nepal and in other countries in Asia; agricultural supplies for indigenous Caribs in Dominica; and medical and other supplies for homeless shelters in Rome. Archbishop Marcinkus listened attentively as I described the many projects that the UNWG had supported in India, China and other parts of Asia; the Middle East; Africa and the Americas. He asked me to send him a list of planned projects so that he could see how he might be able to support our organization. I promised to send him a list, and said: "Thank you, Monsignor, for caring. Our Guild will greatly appreciate your support."

Archbishop Marcinkus then asked me: "What is your religion, Madam President?"

I smiled and answered, "My entire family is Roman Catholic, but please, Monsignor, do not call me Madam President. I am Angela, a simple person who is happy to have an opportunity to be able to help needy children worldwide."

Archbishop Marcinkus answered: "So, Mother Teresa, you and I have something special in common. We all love God and like to do good things! That's nice, Angela!" From then on he called me Angela, and a wonderful bond of mutual respect was built.

I also explained to him that the Prime Minister of the Commonwealth of Dominica, Dame Mary Eugenia Charles, had invited me to be her Ambassador to the Vatican, but that according to Vatican Canon law only a native Dominican could represent the country. He agreed and answered, "Yes, that is what our law says. It's a pity you could not be part of the Diplomatic Corps to the Holy See, however you are always welcome to visit our Vatican family, so come and join us whenever you can – you are always welcome!" He beamed at us with such tremendous energy that he reminded me of Mount Vesuvius, the famous volcano near Naples.

When Monsignor asked my son about his studies, my son told him he was completing his secondary school studies at his boarding school in England and was preparing to take his entrance exams to study at Oxford University. Archbishop Marcinkus congratulated my son and encouraged him to keep it up.

One of the things that impressed me most about Archbishop Marcinkus was his dry sense of humor and his generous laugh as he shared several anecdotes. When we came to talk about his work with the pope, including as his bodyguard, Archbishop Marcinkus told me: "Once I was in Turkey with Pope Paul VI and I was helping a newsman who was interviewing the pope. Later the newsman told me he had been pickpocketed and joked that if he had not seen my hands holding the microphone he would have thought it was me, to which I replied: 'Ah, but did you see the pope's hands?!'"

As we laughed together and we came to speak about his nickname, 'the Gorilla', (because of his build and his bodyguard role), and he went on to joke that when he was told at some point by the media that the church had expanded, he had replied: "So have I!"

However, the archbishop also made it clear that he took his work very seriously. For example, he told me how on one occasion he had given the US Secret Service sixty seconds to get out of the room where US President Nixon was going to meet the pope, or else he would call off the meeting. The archbishop said to me: "Angela, I am always very protective of the pope, the Vatican and of our people here. The Vatican is a sovereign country and our rules must be respected, just as we respect the rules of other countries."

Archbishop Marcinkus continued: "Maybe I am too firm sometimes when I stand up for the Vatican and for what I believe in. One time the media reported widely that I had said: 'You cannot run the Church on Hail Mary's.' But the truth is, when our Vatican employees retire they expect a pension and it is no use telling them I will pay them 400 Hail Mary's. One has to be practical in running a place like this."

When we came to talk about Mother Teresa, my son and I could not help bursting out laughing as Archbishop Marcinkus joked: "Oh, whenever I hear that Mother Teresa is coming, I run the other way!!" He continued: "Seriously, I have tremendous admiration for her. She does a world of good, and one can only admire how incredibly persistent she is when it comes to raising money for her cause, but of course I also have a bank to take care of!"

Years later, at Archbishop Marcinkus' funeral, Bishop Robert Lynch would tell a similar story: on one occasion, while he was visiting Archbishop Marcinkus in Rome, word came in about a surprise visit by Mother Teresa, who wanted to see him. Archbishop Marcinkus had joked: "This visit will cost us a minimum of $1 million!" According to Bishop Lynch, it turned out that Archbishop Marcinkus was right! Mother Teresa was seeking Vatican support for shipping a large donation of mattresses to her Missionaries of Charity. Bishop Lynch would recall that the kind archbishop would always give in to Mother Teresa, adding: "He has now arrived at heaven's gate. I envision Mother Teresa probably still looking for something else he can do for her…"[34]

Given his many responsibilities, I asked the archbishop if he ever relaxed. He said that he did, especially walking through the silent Vatican City or the lovely Vatican gardens early in the morning. He said that sometimes he would be joined by Pope John Paul II, who also liked to take a walk during the early morning hours.

34 Ibid.

Listening to all his stories, I asked him: "Monsignor, have you ever thought of writing a book about all the interesting stories you have told us today?"

"Angela, I would write one if I had the time, especially about our trips to so many countries, although it would probably be only for His Holiness and perhaps the cardinals. Unfortunately I just don't have the time."

"Who knows, Monsignor?" I answered. "Maybe one day I will write a book and tell the readers about all the hilarious stories you told us. Mother Teresa has given me permission to write about her. I believe you are both really inspiring."

"Well, please do so, but be sure to let me have a copy!" Archbishop Marcinkus replied. I promised him that I would. However, a few years later, after completing my work as President of the UNWG, I began to serve the Commonwealth of Dominica as the country's Alternate Permanent Representative to the United Nations agencies in Rome and then, after my husband passed away, I was appointed Dominica's Permanent Representative to the Rome-based United Nations agencies and was also appointed Dominica's Ambassador to the Republic of Italy, in addition to helping frequently with the country's representation in the United States. As I dedicated myself fully to this work for the beautiful Nature Island of Dominica and its wonderful people, I never found the time to keep my promise to write the book, until now.

As he bade us farewell that day, Archbishop Marcinkus reiterated his welcome to visit him at any time and his support for the work of the UNWG.

FOLLOWING OUR FIRST MEETING

Archbishop Marcinkus and I remained in close contact over the years. We spoke many times by telephone, and I met him in his office three times. Each time it was a blessing to listen to him, whether we were talking about Mother Teresa or about his travels with the pope, about helping the poor, or about life and work at the Vatican. Not too long after our initial meeting, I visited the archbishop to hand-deliver an invitation to attend a UNWG event (on 13th May 1981) for the International Year of Disabled Persons. Monsignor Marcinkus had accepted the invitation and intended to attend, but in the end the

Dear Angela.

CHRISTMAS 1982

This has been a year of ups and downs, as you well know. And yet it has been most important because I came to understand the value of friendship in a way that I thought impossible. Friendship is nurtured by love, which in turn depends so much on knowledge of and respect for the loved one. During these past difficult months I have been sustained by the precious ties that bind me to so many people and as a result I have come to appreciate all the more the true meaning of friendship.

The greatest act of friendship, really love, is that shown to us by God in giving His only Son in redemption for all mankind. What an unselfish act of generosity it was and what a treasured gift it still is for all of us! In the light of the coming Holy Year, recalling this tremendous Act of Man's Redemption by Christ, one cannot but be mindful of the new dignity of man saved by the blood of Christ. What thoughts this brings up and how generously responsive we must be to such a marvellous act!

Therefore in love I assure you that, with these thoughts in mind, I have prayed for you at Christmas as I begged the most loving Father to bless you with His choicest gifts.

+ P. Marcinkus

assassination attempt on Pope John Paul II that took place on the very same day made it impossible for him to be there. Archbishop Marcinkus later sent me a check to support the United Nations Women's Guild's projects for needy children. We also corresponded by mail, as can be seen in the warm Christmas greeting that Archbishop Marcinkus sent me at Christmas in 1982.[35]

In 1990, Archbishop Marcinkus called me and told me that he was leaving the Vatican. He told me that he was sad to leave, but that it was better for the pope, the Vatican and his friends. I felt sad. I wished him good luck for his future and told him that I believed in his goodness and would always pray for him. Soon thereafter, I read in the Vatican newspaper that Archbishop Marcinkus had retired from the Vatican, with his good friend Pope John Paul II's full blessings and continuing friendship, and that he had returned to his hometown of Cicero, Illinois. He would later retire to Sun City, Arizona, where he passed away in 2006 at the age of 84.

Maybe Archbishop Marcinkus is now in a special place with his friends Pope John Paul II and Mother Teresa, bringing his great humor to this place. I still smile when I think back to my many laughter-filled conversations with the down-to-earth, humorous, kind giant that the Italian media called 'the Gorilla'. Monsignor Paul Casimir Marcinkus will always remain in my highest esteem. I will never forget the kindness he showed my son McDonald Jr. and me, and his support for the United Nations Women's Guild's work to assist needy children. His resting place is in Cicero, Illinois, next to his parents. May he rest in peace.

---

35 This Christmas greeting for 1982 is just one example of warm and well-wishing exchanges by mail with Archbishop Paul Marcinkus until he called me in 1990 to let me know that he was retiring and moving back to the United States.

CHAPTER X

MEETING MOTHER TERESA FOR THE THIRD TIME

*"Always believe in God. He will be there when you are
in need, because He is a footstep ahead of you."*

Mother Teresa

AT THE NATIONAL PRAYER BREAKFAST WITH MOTHER TERESA

Mother Teresa and I met for the third time in Washington, D.C. in 1994. Although we had remained in contact from time to time over the years, we had not seen each other for some time, so it was very special to be able to bask again–even if only briefly–in the warmth of her friendship.

The occasion was the United States National Prayer Breakfast, held at the Washington Hilton Hotel on 3rd February, 1994. This annual event, which is hosted by Members of Congress each year on the first Thursday of February, originated in the 1950s, and is attended by over 3,000 national and international leaders in politics, diplomacy, religion, business, labor, the arts, and many other spheres of life. The aim is to promote friendship, fellowship and understanding among all citizens in the United States as well as with people from all nations worldwide. President Eisenhower was the first US President to attend a National Prayer Breakfast in 1953, while in 1994, both President Bill Clinton and First Lady Hilary Clinton were present, together with Vice President Al Gore and his wife, Tipper Gore. That year, Mother Teresa was invited to be the guest of honor and she was the keynote speaker at the National Prayer Breakfast.

One of the special invitees at the 1994 National Prayer Breakfast was the Prime Minister of the Commonwealth of Dominica, Dame Mary Eugenia Charles, who was an outstanding and trailblazing leader and the first woman head of government in the Caribbean. In light of my role working for Dominica and my many connections in Washington DC, I had the privilege of being invited to the National Prayer Breakfast together with Dame Charles.

It must have been God's wish to let our table be in the first row below the stage, very close to where Mother Teresa would be seated on the stage. But my first glimpse of her was when she emerged on the stage from behind the curtain to deliver her speech at the podium. With her small, hunched and frail-looking frame, she was barely visible behind the microphones on the podium, but her simple words, imbued with her deep love for all and her faith in Jesus, would reveal an inner strength and power that would move the more than 3,000 people attending the National Prayer Breakfast to their feet in rousing applause.

As I looked up at Mother Teresa at the podium, my heart was pounding with joy and with gratitude to God that Mother Teresa had been invited to address the assembled guests. I listened with bated breath as she started her speech with the prayer of Saint Francis and then went on to speak of the love of Jesus and the importance of every life, with simple words that elicited heartfelt applause from the audience. It was deeply gratifying to listen to her address and to the message of love that she delivered with her humble voice.

Once she had finished speaking, lengthy applause accompanied Mother Teresa as she moved over from the podium to her seat on the right side of the long head table, directly in front of where I was sitting below the stage. I will never be able to express my feelings when Mother Teresa's eyes and mine connected. Friendship and understanding flowed between the two of us in that special moment, even as we were surrounded by thousands of people. Looking at her I folded my hands the Indian way and murmured: "Welcome, Mother Teresa." She smiled at me and lifted her right hand lightly and waved to me.

After the National Prayer Breakfast came to a close, Mother Teresa was taken behind the podium, and I rushed to make certain that I would meet with her. Secret Service officers were stationed at the entrance to the area behind the curtain and wanted to stop me, but I was determined to see my friend, and was able to do so.

Mother Teresa was standing in the hall behind the podium with a few other guests. When she saw me, she came over to me and we held hands for a moment and chatted. After we had greeted each other, asked each other how we were and updated each other, I asked her: "Mother Teresa, please may I have a copy of your speech?" She smiled and said: "Of course!" and turned around to a sister who was accompanying her, who handed her a copy of the speech that Mother Teresa in turn handed over to me.[36]

After I had thanked her, Mother Teresa said: "I will see you in Rome, where we will have much more time."

"Yes, Mother Teresa, I look forward to seeing you there." She smiled at me, held my hands again, and then she had to go. This time our

---

36 The copy of Mother Teresa's speech that she gave me that day, as well as the invitation and program for the National Prayer Breakfast, are attached in the Appendix.

meeting had been only for a few minutes, but it was a happy time and a quality moment for both of us, imbued with sentiments of friendship. It is not important how long a special time is. What is important is to have these moments that one can cherish long afterwards.

CHAPTER XI

SAYING FAREWELL TO MY FRIEND MOTHER TERESA

"I am nothing; I am but an instrument, a tiny pencil in the hands of the Lord with which He writes what He likes. However imperfect we are, He writes beautifully."

Mother Teresa

OUR LAST CONVERSATION

Mother Teresa and I were not able to meet in Rome. In April 1996 she fell from her bed and broke her collarbone, and four months later she contracted a severe bout of malaria that also affected her heart. Her increasingly frail health made it difficult for her to travel. In 1997 she was able to make one final trip to Rome to meet with Pope John Paul II, however she was in Rome for only two days and we were not able to meet.

Although Mother Teresa was too ill to meet with me, she still called me. She told me that she was not feeling well and that she was sorry we could not meet, as we had promised each other at the National Prayer Breakfast in 1994. Mother Teresa told me that she would be flying back to Calcutta the next day. Her voice sounded very weak. I was filled with despair, because I feared that we would not see each other again, nor have a chance to speak with each other again. I told Mother Teresa that I would pray for her and that I wished her a speedy recovery. She thanked me dearly and said: "Angela, friends do not need to see each other always. It is just good to know that they are there." I felt incredibly humble. As I listened to her sincere words of friendship, tears slowly started rolling down my cheeks. She too must have known that we would never meet again, for she shared a few more special words with me that will remain between her and myself forever, before she gave me her blessings and said: "Please take care, Angela."

It was our last telephone call. Alas, I never got to see or speak with Mother Teresa again; however, I shall cherish the final words that we shared in my heart forever.

MY DEAR FRIEND MOTHER TERESA IS CALLED TO GOD

When she returned home to Calcutta, Mother Teresa's health continued to deteriorate, although her dedication and her love for Christ and for all the poorest souls on earth remained unchanged. She had to spend her days in a wheelchair and was not able to travel again. Although she could no longer go out as she had done daily to visit the poor in the slums of Calcutta, she would pray for them and would listen carefully to the sisters of the Missionaries of Charity as they reported about their work. Even though Sister Nirmala had taken over the leadership of the Missionaries of Charity as of March of that year, Mother Teresa continued to provide her loving guidance and advice.

Six months later, on 5th September 1997, Mother Teresa passed away in Calcutta at the age of 87. Her body was transferred to St. Thomas' church, where she lay in state until her funeral one week later.

More than 15,000 people attended her funeral on 13th September 1997. The Indian Government prepared a state funeral for Mother Teresa, and her body was transported from St. Thomas' Church to the Netaji stadium—where her funeral mass was held—on the same gun carriage that had previously borne the bodies of India's luminary leaders Mohandas Gandhi and Jawaharlal Nehru for their respective state funerals. Mother Teresa lay in an open casket with her Rosary wrapped around her hands and surrounded by hundreds of white flowers.

The Vatican's Secretary of State, Cardinal Angelo Sodano, presided over the mass on behalf of Pope John Paul II. The service was attended by royalty, heads of state and of government, members of the church, and dignitaries from more than fifty countries, as well as by the people of Calcutta to whom Mother Teresa had dedicated her life. At the service, Cardinal Sodano delivered a beautiful message from Pope John Paul II for his dear friend, Mother Teresa, which included the following words: "Mother Teresa of Calcutta understood fully this gospel of love. She understood it with every fiber of her indomitable spirit and every ounce of energy of her frail body. She practiced it with all her heart and through the daily toil of her hands, crossing the frontiers of religious and ethnic differences she has taught the world this lesson - it is more blessed to give than to receive."

The Archbishop of Calcutta, Henry D'Souza, added the following beautiful testimony in his eulogy at the service for Mother Teresa: "Dealing with the poor is a divine encounter. The power of Mother Teresa was that she had encountered God in herself, had come to love him and understand his love before she went out to find him in the neighbor... To the dying and the suffering, she brought her tender compassion, washing their wounds, easing their pain. And one of them said so touchingly, 'Mother, so long I have lived as an animal, now I am dying as an angel.'"[37]

Following the state funeral, Mother Teresa's body was placed in its final resting place in a tomb on the ground floor of the Mother-house of the Missionaries of Charity in Calcutta. Archbishop D'Souza presided over the final rites, which were held in private in the presence of the nuns of the Missionaries of Charity. Her crypt has become a place of prayer and pilgrimage for countless visitors inspired by Mother Teresa.[38] Some of Mother Teresa's personal items were later placed on display in a small room next to her crypt, including her two saris, her sandals, her crucifix, handwritten letters she had written, and a five rupee coin given to her long ago by a Jesuit priest in Skopje, which was all she had when she first arrived in Calcutta. In August 2010, the Indian Government released a five-rupee coin to commemorate the 100th Anniversary of the birth of Mother Teresa.[39] I was able to obtain one of the coins and have it with me at all times.

Six years later, in a homily on World Mission Sunday, 19th October, 2003, Mother Teresa's dear friend Pope John Paul II, would state on the occasion of Mother Teresa's beatification: "Let us praise the Lord for this *diminutive woman in love with God*, a humble Gospel messenger and a tireless benefactor of humanity. In her we honor one of the most important figures of our time. Let us welcome her message and follow her example. Virgin Mary, Queen of all the Saints, help us to be gentle

---

37 Pope John Paul II's and Archbishop D'Souza's moving words, which were shared at Mother Teresa's funeral, are quoted in a news report on 13th September, 1997 by the Associated Press for the New York Times, available at http://movies2.nytimes.com/library/world/091397teresa-quotes.html, accessed on 18th November, 2019.

38 See: "Coming on pilgrimage/Visiting Mother Teresa's Tomb, Kolkata", available at https://www.motherteresa.org, accessed on 2nd May 2019.

39 For more information and pictures of the five-rupee coin, see: https://www.mintageworld.com/media/detail/7457-mother-teresa-5-rupee- commemorative-coin/, accessed on 18th November, 2019.

and humble of heart like this fearless messenger of Love. Help us to serve every person we meet with joy and a smile. Help us to be missionaries of Christ, our peace and our hope. Amen!"[40]

FAREWELL, MY DEAR FRIEND

I still remember the moment I learned on CNN that my dear friend, Mother Teresa, had died. I was shocked at first, and then filled with a deep sadness. Tears kept rolling down my cheeks as I listened to the news report. I looked down at my hands, knowing that I would never again feel the warm strength of her fingers curled around mine, and would never walk hand in hand with her again. I went and found a candle and lit it for my friend, and then took my Rosary in my hands and prayed the Rosary for her, as we had done together on our flight from London to Rome.

My dear friend, now you are in Heaven with God, the Blessed Virgin Mary, and with our beloved Jesus, as well as with your friends and loved ones who went before you, and the people whom you had helped. You will also have been joined by now by those called to God after you, including your dear friend Pope John Paul II.

My dear friend, I want you to know that I have not forgotten you and I will never forget you. I keep your miracle medal at my side, but more importantly, I will always hold you in my heart. I will never forget our times together, all our conversations, our understanding for each other, and your special messages for me. I know that you have

---

40 See: Libreria Editrice Vaticana: "Beatification of Mother Teresa of Calcutta: Homily of His Holiness John Paul II," https://www.vatican.va/content/john-paul-ii/en/homilies/2003/documents/hf_jp-ii-hom_20031019_mother-theresa.html, 2003. Accessed on 2nd May 2019.

blessed me. I can still feel how you made the cross on my forehead on the tarmac at Rome's Fiumicino airport. And in recent years, in my moments of poorest health and deepest despair, I have seen you praying for me in heaven and helping me through my ordeals. I will never be able to express how deeply grateful I am that God put you in my life, and that you became my friend.

My dear friend, rest in peace, and may God bless you.

Your humble friend, Angela.

CHAPTER XII

THREE SPECIAL MESSAGES FROM MOTHER TERESA

"Your true character is most accurately measured by how you treat those who can do 'Nothing' for you."

Mother Teresa[41]

More than two decades have passed since Mother Teresa was called to God. During these years I have cherished many fond memories of our friendship, and of being in the presence of a truly

humble soul who saw Jesus in every person and whose mission was to enrich the lives of the poorest people on earth with caring attention, dignity and love. I have reflected at length on her messages, infused as they are

41 Photo credit: Kingkong photo & amp; www. celebrity-photos.com from Laurel Maryland, USA [CC BY-SA 2.0 (https://creativecommons.org/licenses/by-sa/2.0)]; This picture, taken two years before Mother Teresa's passing, is available at: https://commons.wikimedia.org/wiki/File:Mother_Teresa_1.jpg, accessed on 1st June, 2019.

with her love for the poorest, and there are three messages from Mother Teresa that particularly touched my heart and that have guided me in the years since her passing. In closing this brief testament to a dear friendship with Mother Teresa's own words, I wish to share her messages for me with you, the reader, and pray that you may cherish her words and bring them into your life, as I have tried to do in mine.

Whom we should help

"You know, Angela, there is no greater poverty than feeling unwanted. Many of the people whom our Missionaries care for felt unwanted and forgotten by their families and society. Every one wants and deserves to feel loved, and that love should begin in their homes, but it is not always that way. We must begin by sharing love in our homes, but we must not stop there, for everyone is a child of God. We must humbly accept with a grateful heart not only everything that we receive but also every opportunity that we are given to help others."

Mother Teresa

How we can help

"I never think about whether I can help one or two or three people. For me it is important just to be able to help the person in front of me. I can only help one person at a time. Angela, please remember that you can help too. Tell your members at the United Nations Women's Guild and all that you know that we must not try to do big or extraordinary things. We must simply help those who are close to us and put extraordinary love into the little things that we can do for them. Remember that many small acts of love, however small, can make a big change."

Mother Teresa

Final moments in life

"Angela, sometimes it is too late for us to be able to nurse people back to health. The best we can do is to hold their hands and pray at their sides before they are called to God. But this is also important, because people have a right to die with dignity. That can be as simple as knowing that there is someone at their side who cares about them and who gives them love in the final moments of their lives."

Mother Teresa

APPENDIX

MOTHER TERESA'S SPEECH AT THE 1994
NATIONAL PRAYER BREAKFAST

The invitation to the National Prayer Breakfast, held in Washington DC on 3rd February 1994, shows the program of events that day and lists Mother Teresa as the speaker for the "Message", just before the intervention of the President of the United States.

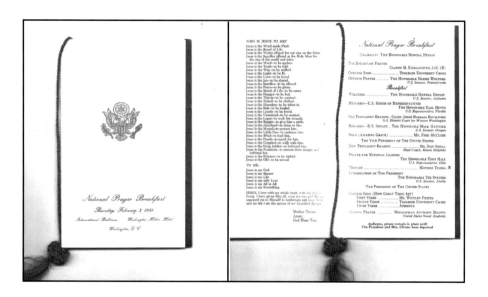

The following four pages show the speech that Mother Teresa delivered that day and are pictures of the actual copy that Mother Teresa gave to me when we met at the end of the National Prayer Breakfast.

WHATEVER YOU DID UNTO ONE OF THE LEAST, YOU DID UNTO ME
Mother Teresa of Calcutta

On the last day, Jesus will say to those on His right hand, "Come, enter the Kingdom. For I was hungry and you gave me food, I was thirsty and you gave me drink, I was sick and you visited me." Then Jesus will turn to those on His left hand and say, "Depart from me because I was hungry and you did not feed me, I was thirsty and you did not give me to drink, I was sick and you did not visit me." These will ask Him, "When did we see You hungry, or thirsty or sick and did not come to Your help?" And Jesus will answer them, "Whatever you neglected to do unto one of the least of these, you neglected to do unto Me!"

As we have gathered here to pray together, I think it will be beautiful if we begin with a prayer that expresses very well what Jesus wants us to do for the least. St. Francis of Assisi understood very well these words of Jesus and His life is very well expressed by a prayer. And this prayer, which we say every day after Holy Communion, always surprises me very much, because it is very fitting for each one of us. And I always wonder whether 800 years ago when St. Francis lived, they had the same difficulties that we have today. I think that some of you already have this prayer of peace - so we will pray it together.

Let us thank God for the opportunity He has given us today to have come here to pray together. We have come here especially to pray for peace, joy and love. We are reminded that Jesus came to bring the good news to the poor. He had told us what is that good news when He said: "My peace I leave with you, My peace I give unto you." He came not to give the peace of the world which is only that we don't bother each other. He came to give the peace of heart which comes from loving - from doing good to others.

And God loved the world so much that He gave His son - it was a giving. God gave His son to the Virgin Mary, and what did she do with Him? As soon as Jesus came into Mary's life, immediately she went in haste to give that good news. And as she came into the house of her cousin, Elizabeth, Scripture tells us that the unborn child - the child in the womb of Elizabeth - leapt with joy. While still in the womb of Mary - Jesus brought peace to John the Baptist who leapt for joy in the womb of Elizabeth.

And as if that were not enough, as if it were not enough that God the Son should become one of us and bring peace and joy while still in the womb of Mary, Jesus also died on the Cross to show that greater love. He died for you and for me, and for that leper and for that man dying of hunger and that naked person lying in the street, not only of Calcutta, but of Africa, and everywhere. Our Sisters serve these poor people in 105 countries throughout the world. Jesus insisted that we love one another as He loves each one of us. Jesus gave His life to love us and He tells us that we also have to give whatever it takes to do good to one another. And in the Gospel Jesus says very clearly: "Love as I have loved you."

Jesus died on the Cross because that is what it took for Him to do good to us - to save us from our selfishness in sin. He gave up everything to do the Father's will - to show us that we too must be willing to give up everything to do God's will - to love one another as He loves each of us. If we are not willing to give whatever it takes to do good to one another, sin is still in us. That is why we too must give to each other until it hurts.

It is not enough for us to say: "I love God," but I also have to love my neighbor. St. John says that you are a liar if you say you love God and you don't love your neighbor. How can you love God whom you do not see, if you do not love your neighbor whom you see, whom you touch, with whom you live? And so it is very important for us to realize that love, to be true, has to hurt. I must be willing to give whatever it takes not to harm other people and, in fact, to do good to them. This requires that I be willing to give until it hurts. Otherwise, there is no true love in me and I bring injustice, not peace, to those around me.

It hurt Jesus to love us. We have been created in His image for greater things, to love and to be loved. We must "put on Christ" as Scripture tells us. And so, we have been created to love as He love us. Jesus makes Himself the hungry one, the naked one, the homeless one, the unwanted one, and He says, "You did it to Me." On the last day He will say to those on His right, "whatever you did to the least of these, you did to Me, and He will also say to those on His left, whatever you neglected to do for the least of these, you neglected to do it for Me."

When He was dying on the Cross, Jesus said, "I thirst." Jesus is thirsting for our love, and this is the thirst of everyone, poor and rich alike. We all thirst for the love of others, that they go out of their way to avoid harming us and to do good to us. This is the meaning of true love, to give until it hurts.

I can never forget the experience I had in visiting a home where they kept all these old parents of sons and daughters who had just put them into an institution and forgotten them - maybe. I saw that in that home these old people had everything - good food, comfortable place, television, everything, but everyone was looking toward the door. And I did not see a single one with a smile on the face. I turned to Sister and I asked: "Why do these people who have every comfort here, why are they all looking toward the door? Why are they not smiling?"

I am so used to seeing the smiles on our people, even the dying ones smile. And Sister said: "This is the way it is nearly every day. They are expecting, they are hoping that a son or daughter will come to visit them. They are hurt because they are forgotten." And see, this neglect to love brings spiritual poverty. Maybe in our own family we have somebody who is feeling lonely, who is feeling sick, who is feeling worried. Are we there? Are we willing to give until it hurts in order to be with our families, or do we put our own interests first? These are the questions we must ask ourselves, especially as we begin this year of the family. We must remember that love begins at home and we must also remember that 'the future of humanity passes through the family.'

I was surprised in the West to see so many young boys and girls given to drugs. And I tried to find out why. Why is it like that, when those in the West have so many more things than those in the East? And the answer was: 'Because there is no one in the family to receive them.' Our children depend on us for everything - their health, their nutrition, their security, their coming to know and love God. For all of this, they look to us with trust, hope and expectation. But often father and mother are so busy they have no time for their children, or perhaps they are not even married or have given up on their marriage. So the children go to the streets and get involved in drugs or other things. We are talking of love of the child, which is where love and peace must begin. These are the things that break peace.

But I feel that the greatest destroyer of peace today is abortion, because it is a war against the child, a direct killing of the innocent child, murder by the mother herself. And if we accept that a mother can kill even her own child, how can we tell other people not to kill one another? How do we persuade a woman not to have an abortion? As always, we must persuade her with love and we remind ourselves that love means to be willing to give until it hurts. Jesus gave even His life to love us. So, the mother who is thinking of abortion, should be helped to love, that is, to give until it hurts her plans, or her free time, to respect the life of her child. The father of that child, whoever he is, must also give until it hurts.

By abortion, the mother does not learn to love, but kills even her own child to solve her problems. And, by abortion, the father is told that he does not have to take any responsibility at all for the child he has brought into the world. That father is likely to put other women into the same trouble. So abortion just leads to more abortion. Any country that accepts abortion is not teaching its people to love, but to use any violence to get what they want. This is why the greatest destroyer of love and peace is abortion.

Many people are very, very concerned with the children of India, with the children of Africa where quite a few die of hunger, and so on. Many people are also concerned about all the violence in this great country of the United States. These concerns are very good. But often these same people are not concerned with the millions who are being killed by the deliberate decision of their own mothers. And this is what is the greatest destroyer of peace today - abortion which brings people to such blindness.

And for this I appeal in India and I appeal everywhere - "Let us bring the child back." The child is God's gift to the family. Each child is created in the special image and likeness of God for greater things - to love and to be loved. In this year of the family we must bring the child back to the center of our care and concern. This is the only way that our world can survive because our children are the only hope for the future. As older people are called to God, only their children are can take their places.

2

But what does God say to us? He says: "Even if a mother could forget her child, I will not forget you. I have carved you in the palm of my hand." We are carved in the palm of His hand; that unborn child has been carved in the hand of God from conception and is called by God to love and to be loved, not only now in this life, but forever. God can never forget us.

I will tell you something beautiful. We are fighting abortion by adoption - by care of the mother and adoption for her baby. We have saved thousands of lives. We have sent word to the clinics, to the hospitals and police stations: "Please don't destroy the child; we will take the child." So we always have someone tell the mothers in trouble: "Come, we will take care of you, we will get a home for your child." And we have a tremendous demand from couples who cannot have a child - but I never give a child to a couple who have done something not to have a child. Jesus said, "Anyone who receives a child in my name, receives me." By adopting a child, these couples receive Jesus but, by aborting a child, a couple refuses to receive Jesus.

Please don't kill the child. I want the child. Please give me the child. I am willing to accept any child who would be aborted and to give that child to a married couple who will love the child and be loved by the child. From our children's home in Calcutta alone, we have saved over 3000 children from abortion. These children have brought such love and joy to their adopting parents and have grown up so full of love and joy.

I know that couples have to plan their family and for that there is natural family planning. The way to plan the family is natural family planning, not contraception. In destroying the power of giving life, through contraception, a husband or wife is doing something to self. This turns the attention to self and so it destroys the gift of love in him or her. In loving, the husband and wife must turn the attention to each other as happens in natural family planning, and not to self, as happens in contraception. Once that living love is destroyed by contraception, abortion follows very easily.

I also know that there are great problems in the world - that many spouses do not love each other enough to practice natural family planning. We cannot solve all the problems in the world, but let us never bring in the worst problem of all, and that is to destroy love. And this is what happens when we tell people to practice contraception and abortion.

The poor are very great people. They can teach us so many beautiful things. Once one of them came to thank us for teaching her natural family planning and said: "You people who have practiced chastity, you are the best people to teach us natural family planning because it is nothing more than self-control out of love for each other." And what this poor person said is very true. These poor people maybe have nothing to eat, maybe they have not a home to live in, but they can still be great people when they are spiritually rich.

When I pick up a person from the street, hungry, I give him a plate of rice, a piece of bread. But a person who is shut out, who feels unwanted, unloved, terrified, the person who has been thrown out of society - that spiritual poverty is much harder to overcome. And abortion, which often follows from contraception, brings a people to be spiritually poor, and that is the worst poverty and the most difficult to overcome.

Those who are materially poor can be very wonderful people. One evening we went out and we picked up four people from the street. And one of them was in a most terrible condition. I told the Sisters: "You take care of the other three; I will take care of the one who looks worse." So I did for her all that my love can do. I put her in bed, and there was such a beautiful smile on her face. She took hold of my hand, as she said one word only: "thank you" - and she died.

I could not help but examine my conscience before her. And I asked: "What would I say if I were in her place?" And my answer was very simple. I would have tried to draw a little attention to myself. I would have said: "I am hungry, I am dying, I am cold, I am in pain," or something. But she gave me much more - she gave me her grateful love. And she died with a smile on her face. Then there was the man we

3

picked up from the drain, half eaten by worms and, after we had brought him to the home, he only said, "I have lived like an animal in the street, but I am going to die as an angel, loved and cared for." Then, after we had removed all the worms from his body, all he said, with a big smile, was: "Sister, I am going home to God" -and he died. It was so wonderful to see the greatness of that man who could speak like that without blaming anybody, without comparing anything. Like and angel - this is the greatness of people who are spiritually rich even when they are materially poor.

We are not social workers. We may be doing social work in the eyes of some people, but we must be contemplatives in the heart of the world. For we must bring that presence of God into your family, for the family that prays together, stays together. There is so much hatred, so much misery, and we with our prayer, with our sacrifice, are beginning at home. Love begins at home, and it is not how much we do, but how much love we put into what we do.

If we are contemplatives in the heart of the world with all its problems, these problems can never discourage us. We must always remember what God tells us in Scripture: "Even if a mother could forget the child in her womb - something impossible, but even if she could forget - I will never forget you.

And so here I am talking with you. I want you to find the poor here, right in your own home first. And begin love there. Ben that good news to your own people first. And find out about your next-door neighbors. Do you know who they are?

I had the most extraordinary experience of love of neighbor with a Hindu family. A gentleman came to our house and said: "Mother Teresa, there is a family who have not eaten for so long. Do something." So I took some rice and went there immediately. And I saw the children - their eyes shining with hunger. I don't know if you have every seen hunger. But I have seen it very often. And the mother of the family took the rice I gave her and went out. When she came back, I asked her: "Where did you go? What did you do?" And she gave me a very simple answer: "They are hungry also." What struck me was that she knew - and who are they? A Muslim family - and she knew. I didn't bring any more rice that evening because I wanted them, Hindus and Muslims, to enjoy the joy of sharing.

But there were those children, radiating joy, sharing the joy and peace with their mother because she had the love to give until it hurts. And you see this is where love begins - at home in the family.

So, as the example of this family shows, God will never forget us and there is something you and I can always do. We can keep the joy of loving Jesus in our hearts, and share that joy with all we come in contact with. Let us make that one point - that no child will be unwanted, unloved, uncared for, or killed and thrown away. And give until it hurts - with a smile.

Because I talk so much of giving with a smile, once a professor from the United States asked me: "Are you married?" And I said: "Yes, and I find it sometimes very difficult to smile at my spouse, Jesus, because He can be very demanding - sometimes." This is really something true. And there is where love comes in - when it is demanding, and yet we can give it with joy.

One of the most demanding things for me is travelling everywhere - and with publicity. I have said to Jesus that if I don't go to heaven for anything else, I will be going to heaven for all the travelling with all the publicity, because it has purified me and sacrificed me and made me really ready to go to heaven.

If we remember that God loves us, and that we can love others as He loves us, then America can become a sign of peace for the world. From here, a sign of care for the weakest of the weak - the unborn child - must go out to the world. If you become a burning light of justice and peace in the world, then really you will be true to what the founders of this country stood for. God bless you!

####

REFERENCES

Associated Press. "Quotes From Mother Teresa's Funeral Service", available at: http://movies2.nytimes.com/library/world/091397 teresa-quotes.html, accessed on 18th November, 2019.

Benenate, Becky, and Joseph Durepos, Editors. "Mother Teresa: No Greater Love", published by MJF Books, New York, 1997.

Biema, David. "Mother Teresa: The Life and Works of a Modern Saint", a Time Magazine Special Edition published by Time Inc. Books, New York, 2016.

Castor, Helen. "Joan of Arc: A History", published by HarperCollins Publishers, New York, 2015.

Catholic Hierarchy. "Archbishop Paul Casimir Marcinkus", available at: http://www.catholic-hierarchy.org/bishop/bmarcp.html, accessed on 29th March, 2019.

Catholic Online. "St. Francis of Assisi", available at: https://www.catholic.org/saints/saint.php?saint_id=50, accessed on 31st May, 2019.

Collopy, Michael. "Works of Love are Works of Peace: Mother Teresa of Calcutta and the Missionaries of Charity", published by Ignatius Press, San Francisco, 1996.

Gallagher, Jim. "Mother Teresa", published by the Catholic Truth Society, available at: https://issuu.com/catholictruthsociety/docs/b. mother teresa, accessed on 7th May, 2019.

King, Heather. "Jacqueline de Decker", published by the Catholic Education Resource Center, available at: https://www.catholic education.org/en/faith-and-character/faith-and-character/jacqueline-de-decker.html, accessed on 14th May, 2019.

Langford, Joseph. "Mother Teresa's Secret Fire", published by Our Sunday Visitor, Huntingdon IN, 2008.

Libreria Editrice Vaticana. "Beatification of Mother Teresa of Calcutta: Homily of His Holiness John Paul II", available at: http://w2.vatican.va/content/john-paul-ii/en/homilies/2003/documents/hf jp-ii hom 20031019 mother-theresa.html, 2003, accessed on 2nd May, 2019.

Mintage World. "Mother Teresa 5 Rupee Commemorative Coin", available at: https://www.mintageworld.com/media/detail/7457-mother-teresa-5-rupee-commemorative-coin/, 2018, accessed on 18th November, 2019.

Mother Teresa Center of the Missionaries of Charity. "Statistics 2015", available at: https://motherteresa.org, accessed on 27th March, 2019.

Mother Teresa of Calcutta Center. "Coming on pilgrimage/Visiting Mother Teresa's Tomb, Kolkata", available at: https://www.mother teresa.org, accessed on 2nd May, 2019.

Muggeridge, Malcolm. "Something Beautiful for God: Mother Teresa of Calcutta", published by Harper & Row, Publishers, San Francisco, 1971.

Pope John Paul II. "Love is the Explanation of Everything: 365 Meditations with the Pope", published by Rizzoli International Publications, New York, 2011.

Ramirez, Margaret. "A final farewell for 'God's Banker'", Chicago Tribune, available at: https://www.chicagotribune.com/news/ct-xpm-2006-03-03-0603030276-story.html, accessed on 29th March, 2019.

Rezac, Mary. "The beautiful meeting of John Paul II and Mother Teresa", Catholic Online, available at: https://www.catholic.org/news/hf/faith/story.php?id=71527, accessed on 27th March, 2019.

St. Bonaventure. "The life of St. Francis of Assisi", published by Tan Books, Charlotte, North Carolina, 2010.

St. Thérèse of Lisieux: "The Story of a Soul: the Autobiography of The Little Flower", published by Saint Benedict Press, Charlotte, North Carolina, 1990.

Spink, Kathryn. "Mother Teresa *(Revised and Updated)*: An Authorised Biography", published by HarperCollins, New York, 2011.

Van Biema, David. "Mother Teresa: The Life and Works of a Modern Saint", an Updated Reissue of Time's Special Edition, published by Time Magazine, 2016.

Williamson, Allen. "Biography of Joan of Arc", available at: http://archive.joan-of-arc.org, accessed on 1st June, 2019.